THE STATE AND
THE CITIZEN

AN INTRODUCTION TO
POLITICAL PHILOSOPHY

J. D. Mabbott
Formerly President of St John's College, Oxford

HUTCHINSON UNIVERSITY LIBRARY
LONDON

HUTCHINSON & CO (*Publishers*) LTD
178-202 Great Portland Street, London W1

London Melbourne Sydney
Auckland Johannesburg Cape Town

First published 1948
Reprinted 1952, 1955, 1956, 1958,
1961, 1962, 1963, 1965
Second edition 1967
Reprinted 1970

This book has been set in Times, printed in Great Britain
by offset-litho on Smooth Wove paper by Anchor Press, and
bound by Wm. Brendon, both of Tiptree, Essex
ISBN 0 09 043301 7 (cased)
0 09 043302 5 (paper)

CONTENTS

PREFACE

In this book I attempt to bring out the general principles of politics. Any such attempt meets with two difficulties. Firstly, it is not easy to separate political philosophy from social psychology, from economic organisation, and from the historical study of political institutions. The reader may well expect to find Group Personality, Communism, Democracy, Representative Government and International Organisation fully discussed here. If so, he will be disappointed. The reasons for these omissions are indicated in the Appendix. The second difficulty is that a political philosopher may be tempted to regard the peculiarities of his own civilisation (e.g. of 'Western Democracy') as permanent principles, when they are only local prejudices. On this, I can only say that I have tried to show that the principles are permanent by giving the arguments for them. In politics, as in ethics, I cannot agree that local variation in standards must involve relativity in values. This does not mean that the principles here defended are immediately applicable or should be immediately imposed all over the world. It may even be the case that only in Western Europe, in the British Commonwealth, and in the United States of America have historical conditions been such as to make their application possible within any foreseeable future. Nevertheless, if the Balkans or China or the USSR are debarred, for the present or the indefinite future, from following or even from recognising these principles (by reason of their historical development, their moral traditions or their special local difficulties), I cannot avoid the conclusion that, in the field of politics at least, they are condemned to lasting loss and sacrifice.

My debts are mainly obvious. However much I have diverged from their conclusions, I have found in the writings of T. H. Green and B. Bosanquet an invaluable starting-point for modern political theory. I regret that I did not have the chance of seeing *States and Morals* by T. D. Weldon before completing my own work. Though our methods diverge and some of our conclusions differ, I believe we are discussing the same problems and regard them as important for the same reasons. I have been helped by the generations of my pupils and above all by Mr M. B. Foster, who read most of this book in manuscript and has enabled me to clear up some of the obscurities in it.

J.D.M.

St John's College, Oxford
December 1947

(A)
From Hobbes to Hegel

I

THE USE OF AUTHORITIES

The aim of this book is to work through partial and one-sided theories of political obligation towards a more complete view. In the present section the chapters entitled with the names of Hobbes, Locke, Rousseau and Hegel do not attempt to be fair and exhaustive accounts of the views of the philosophers concerned, still less to provide a history of the subject. They select points of permanent value and interest with the aim of advancing the enquiry.

This method may require a word of defence. Why not omit the more partial or erroneous views? No scientist would devote chapter after chapter to the phlogiston or the flat earth theory when he knew the right, or even a better, answer. It is just here, however, that science and philosophy part company.

The philosopher does not discover new facts. His concern is our everyday view with its common landmarks, duty, obedience, law, desire. He does not set out, as the scientist does, grasping his compass, towards lands no man has trod, nor return thence bearing strange treasures and stranger tales. He is rather to be pictured ascending the tower of some great cathedral, such as St Stephen's, Vienna. As he goes up the spiral stairway, the common and particular details of life, the men and tramcars, shrink to invisibility and the big landmarks shake themselves clear. Little windows open at his elbow with widening views. There is conscience; over there is duty; there is conscience again looking quite different from this new level; now he is high enough to see law and liberty from one window.

And ever there haunts him the vision of the summit, where there is a little room with windows all round, where he may recover his breath and see the view as a whole, and the Schottenkirche and the Palace of Justice in their true relative proportions, and where that gargoyle (determinism, was it?) which loomed in on him so menacingly at one stage in his ascent shall have shrunk to the speck that it is.

We shall be told that no one reaches the top. A philosopher who ceases to climb does so only because he gets tired; and he remains crouched against some staircase window, commanding but a dusty and one-sided view at best, obstinately proclaiming to the crowds below, who do not listen, that he is at the summit and can see the whole city. That may be so. Yet the climb itself is not without merit for those whose heads can stand the height and the circling of the rising spiral; and, even at the lowest windows, one is above the smoke and can see proportions more clearly so that men and tramcars can never look quite the same again.

Moreover, Hobbes, Locke and Rousseau are no strangers. The modern citizen of a western State carries them with him. He is ineluctably Hobbes when he reads of the state of Palestine or remembers the Ireland of 1922. He is Locke when he suspends his thinking and falls back on the contradictory catchwords of all his favourite newspapers. He is Rousseau when his imagination runs away with him and he reconciles these contradictions by short cuts to Utopia. But he is in no danger of becoming John of Salisbury; and the essentials of Plato and Aristotle are so embedded in Greek life and City State that they cannot serve as companions in the first stages of such a quest as this.

2

HOBBES

Three main factors determine the problems of political theory as they come to us today; nationality, individualism and specialisation. It is because Hobbes was the first political theorist to recognise all three that his work may fitly open our enquiry.

Firstly, then, we have that youthful experiment, the nation. In the <u>middle ages political authority was dispersed and divided; and much now thought of as political was claimed by the Church.</u> Ties of varying strength, and none clearly political, attached a man to his guild, city, abbey, manor, baron, king and pope. If you met an Englishman in the street in the fourteenth century and asked him what his country did for him and what he owed to her, he might well be nonplussed. No one did anything for him, but he certainly owed a week's service annually to the baron and eggs to the abbey and so on. Two centuries later he would have known the answer, for by that time political authority had crystallised in the nation.

> Oh, when shall Englishmen
> With such acts fill a pen
> Or England breed again
> Such a King Harry?

It is true that this spirit was born in battle, during the great contests with France. It is true also that, though nations appeared so early, nationality was not explicitly recognised as the basis of State unity until 1919. As nations were born in war, so until the

treaties of Trianon and Versailles emphasised nationality in
frontier-drawing, their limits were set by conquest and their
authority enforced by arms. We puzzled our early Englishman
by questions about his 'country'; we might equally have puzzled
a Czech or a Pole in 1900.

In the second place we put individualism, the growth of free
criticism, the religious idea dominating the Reformation, that the
individual soul is of primary importance, and that by their effect
and value for men shall institutions and ritual and priests be
judged. The idea was religious, but a gospel of liberty soon
widens its range, and when the Church has been attacked the
King cannot escape. Nor can he stand on divine sanctions or
historical precedents when these have failed his greater cousin
in Rome.

Thirdly, there is the specialisation of institutions. Never before
had political authority been clearly separated from divine authority. Like the City State, Rome and the Church had been 'universal
providers'. The medieval town nestles under its cathedral and its
cathedral was its concert room, its museum, its art gallery and its
music hall. Rome rendered wonderful service in keeping all these
torches alight during the dark ages, but specialisation brings
strength. By Hobbes' time all these activities had grown, in
England at least, their own institutions. Secular science had produced Gilbert and Harvey; secular drama had found a Shakespeare within fifty years of its birth; secular education was flower-
ing in the grammar schools, secular art and music were finding
new subjects and new patrons. The strength of autonomy was
infused into the State also, and the political theorist was given
his problem clear. Just as irrelevant religious considerations were
ruled out from the questions 'What is scientific truth?', 'What
are subjects for art?', so also the appeal to revelation or divine
authority disappears from politics. Here too Hobbes was a
pioneer.

The paradox of politics is the reconciliation of liberty and
obligation, and a first free enquiry might naturally light on
Contract as a parallel. A contract is freely made but binds its
maker; it gives him something of value but at a stated cost. Hobbes
casts his political theory into the contract form. He tells us that
men were once unsocial, but that they suffered so intensely from
the insecurity of this isolated life that they made a contract with
each other to give up their rights to a sovereign, some man or
assembly of men, who should have power to keep the peace and

guarantee their security. To this, some of Hobbes' critics thought it sufficient to answer that the contract is a myth, that the state of nature never existed nor did men ever give up their rights to a sovereign, that in any case the descent of the sovereignty had often been broken on the sovereign's side and that on the subjects' side the original contractors could not bind their descendants. An amusing specimen of this difficulty in the historical claim is to be found in Edward I's letter to Pope Boniface VIII, in which he lays claim to the throne of Scotland. 'About the time of Eli and the prophet Samuel, a certain man of the Trojan race, Brut by name, a man of vigour and distinction, after the fall of Troy, put in with many Trojan nobles at a certain island then called Albion and inhabited only by giants.' Tracing his line from this source Edward I concludes that 'it is evident that the throne of Scotland belongs to us in full right'.[1]

The right reply, however, to such historical forms of the contract theory is not that Hobbes' history is wrong but that all such history is irrelevant. My obligation to my country cannot be decided one way or the other by the putative activities of a number of missing links huddled round the altars of Stonehenge.

This irrelevance of origin to value causes much difficulty. At all times men have looked for a lofty origin for what they revere. A Greek city must have a hero-founder with a divine parent, and it was this necessity which populated the Greek pantheon and dictated the amours of its members. Even now when science finds the origin of man among the apes or the fishes, or traces morality to taboo, religion to superstition, the Mass to assimilative theophagy, all these discoveries seem to the moralist and the theologian a degradation of their temples. They think the scientist will go on to draw the conclusion that religion is mere superstition and morality nothing but taboo. But this is only their own fallacy turned upside down and the scientist is no more likely to commit himself to these dogmas than to the assertion 'man is merely a fish'. If 'evolution' has any meaning at all, the origin of a thing will never explain it or determine or delimit its value. However society may have originated, its origins are of no significance whatever for political theory.

The contract theory, however, does not lose its value by losing its historical accuracy. Hobbes' story is a myth, and a myth may be a good myth even if its dates are wrong. Archbishop

1. *Annales Londinienses*. Stubbs' Edition of the Chronicles of Edward I and Edward II, vol. I, pp. 113–120.

Ussher dated the Creation on 7 September 4004 B.C.; but a
modern theologian, when he speaks of the Fall, refers to characteristics of man's present nature and not to a historical event near
Baghdad. His views cannot therefore be shaken by ruins in Crete
or footprints in the Lower Carboniferous. When the Greek
demoralised his gods in order to obtain a hero-founder this was
simply his imaginative way of saying, 'My city embodies something superhuman and divine—and is just as good as yours.'

Hobbes is really aware that his story is a myth. For when he
is pressed to answer the question, 'Why do I obey the sovereign?'
he replies that unless I and the other citizens did so there would
be a state of war in the land. Further, I am entitled to rebel when
the power of the sovereign is not strong enough to protect me.
The contract on which my obedience rests is clearly one between
me and the other citizens; and the sovereign whom our contract
sets up is her reigning Majesty in parliament and not some
palaeolithic Brut or Ug. If we want to find the state of nature
we do not go back in history; we perform a logical abstraction.
We remove from human life what government provides and we
see what would be left.

We must therefore restate Hobbes' myth, as modern theology
restates Genesis, and as Hobbes himself really intended. It will
then run somewhat as follows. Man is by nature—that is, by
instinct and desire—a selfish individual. His reason leads him to
accept State control and social life as a necessary evil to avoid
greater evils. These greater evils centre round fear. The State's
only function therefore is to provide security by keeping the peace.
In order to make quite sure of this, the government must have
very extensive powers. It must command the army and control
the executive, look after finance and education, enforce religious
uniformity, and control moral and scientific teaching. There is
only the one limitation noted above. The sovereign has no right
to threaten my life. If, through his overt act or through his growing
weakness, my security is endangered I am free from all obligation.
Here is obviously a very different atmosphere from the historical
and legal one which met us at the first glance. Within his premisses Hobbes' logic is unrelenting, and it is by criticism of his
premisses alone that we can query his conclusions and advance
our enquiry.

The first ground of criticism is found in Hobbes' individualism.
'Man is by nature a social animal.' Hobbes was well aware of
Aristotle's dictum, and asked, in reply: 'Do the social animals

quarrel among themselves over wealth or precedence? Do the bees rebel against their queen? Do the wasps spend half their time making complicated arrangements to sting each other? Do the ants lock up their houses when they take the air?' The obvious answers to these questions confirmed him in his belief that only fear and cold calculation drive men into society and keep them there. There seems little doubt, however, that both Hobbes and Aristotle were wrong. Man is certainly not a social animal in the full sense; yet when we look for the bonds of social life we cannot make them entirely rational. The social instinct, which makes solitary confinement the most terrible punishment of all, which drives holiday-makers to football matches, and which in the evenings fills one street in a town to overflowing while the others are deserted—this is a force which no politician or political theorist can neglect. 'If eating and drinking be natural, herding is so too.'[1] But the social instinct is only one among others and is at best intermittent in its activity, and in some people wholly ineffective. It is almost as insufferable to many men to be never alone as to be always alone, and 'the Englishman's house is his castle' is as natural an expression of the English character as are all our little clubs and societies. Yet the gregarious instinct is certainly one force among others in human nature, and Hobbes was wrong to omit it entirely.

The next objection to Hobbes is that he makes society and law precede morality. It is held that this is actually a false position and that it leads Hobbes into self-contradiction. We must reserve for a later occasion the main issue, whether or not morality is a social product and how far laws are made and not discovered by the sovereign (Chapter 9), but we can defend Hobbes against his literal critics on the second point. They point to Hobbes' view that contracts are 'words and breath' without a sovereign to enforce them, that morality is what the sovereign commands. They then ask, 'What of the original contract?' It at least implies no power to enforce it and suggests a pre-social trust and morality. This, however, is not the case. The force behind the original contract is exactly that behind all others—the sovereign; and the men who make the contract need not be moved by sociability or moral motives. They may be using their fellow men and the sovereign merely as tools to further a particular private end. Suppose I want to take exercise, and I decide that exercise taken with other people has merits, either competitive or financial. I

1. Shaftesbury.

pay a subscription to a club and allow a man or body of men
to make rules which limit my activity in hundreds of ways. It is
clear that my motives throughout might be entirely selfish. We
have been insisting above that the motive is not entirely selfish,
but there is no internal contradiction in Hobbes' theory that it is.
We now come to the contract itself, to the purchase and its
price. The purchase is security. Is this all we need to ask from
the State? It is often pointed out that fear was obviously a very
real motive to Hobbes. His exits and entrances when English
politics required them, his own confessions, the evidence of his
style, which always rises to its finest when he utters warnings of
war—all these show us how highly he valued security. To some
men, however, fear of death is not so dominant a motive, and
they are just the men who give a government trouble—the rebel,
the martyr, the duellist, the gangster, the highwayman. There are
goods, such as freedom of thought or conscience, for which lives
have been risked; and Hobbes' attempt to crush them in the
interests of peace would threaten peace rather than secure it.
In support of this criticism, two passages in Hobbes himself
may be quoted which seem to allow that the State has wider
ends than mere security. In his description of the state of nature,
the well-known peroration occurs: 'there is no place for industry;
because the fruit thereof is uncertain: and consequently no
culture of the earth, no navigation, nor use of the commodities
that may be imported by sea; no commodious building; no
instruments of moving and removing such things as require much
force; no knowledge of the face of the earth; no account of time;
no Arts; no Letters; no Society; and, which is worst of all,
continuall feare, and danger of violent death and the life of man
solitary, poore, nasty, brutish, and short.'[1] The State comes
admittedly to remove the last great evil; should it not secure for
man the goods which the state of nature lacks? The answer seems
to be given later in the book. 'The office of the sovereign consisteth
in . . . the procuration of the safety of the people. . . . But by
safety here is not meant a bare preservation, but also all other
contentments of life which every man by lawfull industry without
danger or hurt to the commonwealth shall acquire to himselfe.'[2]
Once again the critic may think he has caught Hobbes in a self-
contradiction, but this is not so. Hobbes is saying that the only
duty of the sovereign is to keep the peace. If he does that he
makes possible the citizen's own pursuit of other goods. There

1. *Leviathan*, ch. XIII.   2. Ib., ch. XXX.

is no suggestion that the State should assist in the pursuit of these other goods; it need only secure the citizen in his activity and possession. Thus in one sense Hobbes' sovereign is not nearly absolute enough. All his powers are directed to security. His only interest in religion or education is a security interest. Let the government keep the peace and let the citizens provide all other goods for themselves. We should think little of a modern government which concerned itself with nothing more than the protection of the lives and limbs of the citizens. Hobbes' view of the *functions* of the State is a minimal view, though the *powers* he attributes to the sovereign, as required to perform these functions, may be maximum powers. But they would still stop far short of the powers daily exercised by any modern State. Hobbes' sovereign would take no interest in the promotion of health or education. He would permit the citizen to achieve these ends by his own efforts within the framework of order and security provided by the State. Even this permissive attitude, however, is abandoned if the pursuit of any such private end brings 'danger or hurt to the Commonwealth'. We may think Hobbes' attitude to religion —to take the most striking example—is intolerable, but it is not far removed from the attitude of every sovereign. If a religious body instigates its members to break the peace, the police will rightly intervene. It is true of course that sectarian differences are not usually settled by appeals to arms, as they were in Hobbes' day, but this only means that he had some justification in taking his stronger line. Where, as in Ireland, ordeal by battle still has attractions, the sovereign still 'tramples on religious liberty', forbidding inhabitants of Belfast even to utter in public their wishes concerning the Pope. We may also say that history teaches that enforced uniformity encourages resistance, but once again we are differing from Hobbes only about ways and means, and agreeing with him on fundamentals.

Perhaps the most significant difference is that we await danger, but Hobbes anticipates it. With us the police interfere when the rioting begins; Hobbes introduces oppressive legislation to obviate even the risk of rioting. Here again we agree that peace is essential. With a strong and dispersed police force, with a fairly civilised populace, with religious leaders addicted more to newspaper controversy than to torture, the modern sovereign is able to rely on *ad hoc* measures when the need occurs. Hobbes, with no police and a populace addicted to fighting, and especially to fighting about religion, was surely justified in stronger action. To the main point that the sovereign's primary duty is to ensure peace we must recur in the next chapter.

Security, then, is the purchase in our social contract. The price is absolutism. Here once again Hobbes has drawn inaccurate critics into unjustified antagonism. To say the sovereign is absolute is in one sense simply tautology. There are things he will not do because they would lessen his authority, but from his decision there is no appeal, and against him there is only one remedy: rebellion. This insistence on the legal and constitutional absolutism of the sovereign has been of great importance for English jurisprudence, which descends directly from Hobbes through Austin. A rival theory, the 'sovereignty of the people', with its divided powers and 'checks and balances', veiled for centuries from political thinkers the trenchant certainty of Hobbes. While this question can have only a passing reference here, we can at least clear up a confusion which has side-tracked superficial critics of Hobbes. Absolutism tends to suggest monarchy, with which it has nothing whatever to do. It is true that Hobbes personally thought monarchy the simplest and safest type of government, but that is not the essence of his political theory. Throughout the general chapters of his work even his own personal view does not make him forget to write 'the sovereign (be it a monarch or an assembly)'. Except in *Leviathan*, ch. XIX, which discusses the relative merits of types of government, the word 'assembly' can be written in everywhere after the word 'sovereign' without affecting the argument at all. It is curious how many people would then be reconciled to the absolutism which has remained all along unaltered.[1]

1. *Note.* Cf. Pref. to *Philosophical Rudiments* (Works [1837] vol. II, p. xxii), where Hobbes makes it his rule 'not to seem of opinion that there is less proportion of obedience due to an aristocracy or democracy than a monarchy. For tho' I have endeavoured by arguments in my tenth chapter to gain a belief in men that monarchy is the most commodious government, which one thing alone I confess in this whole book not to be demonstrated but only probably stated; yet everywhere I expressly say that in all kind of government whatever there ought to be a supreme and equal power.'

3

LOCKE

It is customary to regard Locke as the second of the three classical authorities, through whom our subject develops from its priest-ridden beginnings to its democratic goal. His work in political theory, however, is not to be compared with that of Hobbes and Rousseau, and his perennial popularity is an exact measure of the accuracy with which he reflects the muddled condition of an ordinary man who has suddenly been faced with the problem of political authority. Yet from this confusion we may extract for our own purposes three views of the nature of political obligation which are all of real importance.

Firstly, however, we must deal briefly with Locke's attack on Hobbes. Though he never names his great contemporary, he refers to some persons who had gone so far as to confuse the state of nature and the state of war, when the one is 'a state of peace, goodwill, mutual assistance and preservation' and the other 'a state of enmity, malice, violence and mutual destruction'.[1] It is clear at once that out of Locke's state of nature no society could ever arise. If men 'naturally'—i.e. without restraint—would re-frain from theft and violence and respect their neighbours' rights, we should never need judges nor a policeman at the corner of the street. As usual Locke has another and a diametrically op-posed conception of the state of nature which meets this objection. 'The pravity of mankind being such that they had rather injuri-ously prey upon the fruits of other men's labours than take pains to provide for themselves, the necessity of preserving men in what

1. *Second Treatise on Civil Government*, ch. III, para. 19.

honest industry has acquired . . . obliges men to enter into
society with one another.'[1] Locke seems not only to be wholly
unaware of the violent self-contradiction here but also to be
blind to the fact that the second and only adequate theory of the
state of nature (that it is an 'ill condition', 'full of fears and
continual dangers') is identical with that of Hobbes. For Hobbes
insists that when he says a state of nature is a state of war he
does not mean by 'war' continual fighting, but insecurity and un-
certainty. 'For as the nature of Foule weather, lyeth not in a
showre or two of rain; but in an inclination thereto of many
dayes together; so the nature of war, consisteth not in actual
fighting; but in the known disposition thereto, during all the time
there is no assurance to the contrary.'[2] Here then the attempt
to state Locke's position has simply revealed his surrender to
Hobbes, and reinforced the conclusion we drew from him that the
primary need of a people and its first demand from a government
is security for life and limb. If this is not the only need of a people,
it is the most important, because (as Hobbes saw) only security
makes possible the pursuit of any further civilised aim whatever.
This is the answer to the argument above that Hobbes overrates
the desire for security as a human motive, that many men are
ready to risk security for greater goods. This may be so with
individual men but it must not be so with governments. Any
government which says 'We place health or education or religious
liberty above security' contradicts itself. Any attempt to develop
health or education or religious toleration while at the same time
troubling little about security would defeat its own ends.

Security may not be the highest political end but it is the
necessary basis for the achievement of any other political end;
and therefore the first claim on government. This achievement of
the State is usually forgotten by its citizens because it is taken
for granted. They make plans for next week, they go home safely
through the streets after dark, they cycle across an open moor;
and they never give a thought to the organisation which ensures
these conditions. The only way to convince a Golden Age theorist
of Locke's type is to ask him to conduct a business in a State
where the legal system is corrupt, to take a journey through
mountains where there are brigands, to go and live in a city or
country where authority has disappeared. If he is allowed to

1. *A Letter concerning Toleration* (Works [1823] vol. VI, p. 42). See also
Second Treatise, ch. IX, paras. 123, 127.
2. *Leviathan*, ch. XIII.

fight with the other temporarily noble savages he may be fairly
happy; but, if the country is in a state not of 'battle' but of 'war',
he will soon discover the meaning and the prescience of Hobbes'
gloomy imaginings. I lived for a month in Ireland in 1922. There
was no actual loss of life near us during that time, only a few
shots audible in the night. Yet there were fear and suspicion
everywhere and all peaceful avocations had come to an end. Fear
and veiled hostility had destroyed the whole structure of social
life. No doubt every man is not naturally and constantly a would-
be murderer or thief, but Locke forgot that the bad men do not
go about labelled for our benefit; and (as Hobbes pointed out)
every man who locks his house when he goes for a walk lays mankind under the same general accusation.

   Hobbes' theory may be said to follow from his low and cynical
view of human nature as essentially individualist. Locke's opposed
view of human nature as essentially sociable, friendly and co-
operative is a natural reaction. The truth, of course, lies between
the two. Some men are sociable and some are anti-social. In
every man the two elements are so mixed that either may on
occasion come uppermost. But Hobbes' theory of the state of
nature remains unshaken by this compromise. For the existence
in any society of a few bad men (especially when their identity
and whereabouts are unknown), and the known existence of an
anti-social 'streak' in every man, would combine to cause the
'State of War' which Hobbes describes. In 1928 I came across two
valleys in Rumania where all civilised activities had ceased,
owing to the presence of a band of brigands. Markets were
empty, fields untilled, houses barricaded. The terrorised population must have numbered some thousands. The brigands were
finally rounded up by the Army; they numbered thirty-five.

   De Quincey's account (in *Murder as One of the Fine Arts*) of
the impression created by John Williams, and Coleridge's attitude
to it, are relevant here. John Williams had practically wiped out
two families. 'It would be absolutely impossible adequately to
describe the frenzy of feelings which, throughout the next fort-
night, mastered the popular heart. . . . For twelve succeeding
days, under some groundless notion that the unknown murderer
had quitted London, the panic which had convulsed the mighty
metropolis diffused itself all over the island. I was myself at that
time nearly 300 miles from London; but there, and everywhere,
the panic was indescribable. . . . Women more than once died
upon the spot from the shock of attending some suspicious

intrusion upon the part of vagrants, meditating probably nothing worse than a robbery, but whom the poor women . . . had fancied to be the dreadful London murderer. . . . Coleridge, whom I saw some months after these terrific murders, told me that for *his* part, though at the time resident in London, he had not shared in the prevailing panic: *him* they affected only as philosopher, and threw him into a profound reverie upon the tremendous power which is laid open in a moment to a man who can reconcile himself to the adjuration of all conscientious restraints, if, at the same time, thoroughly without fear.'

So we come to the three answers Locke gives to the problem of sovereignty. The first is a survival of the Noble Savage and his Golden Age. In the state of nature man would be perfect, he would respect his neighbours' rights and hear and obey the voice of reason within him. All he needs is to be left alone. It is true that he fears those depraved persons his suspicion of whom makes the age less golden, but all the State need do is to keep them in check. This first theory is individualism and it is one of Locke's most endearing characteristics. Nobody likes to be interfered with, and there is therefore a uniformly popular trend in political theory which separates the spheres of liberty and restraint, and then, enlarging the one and narrowing the other, reaches the conclusion that a State comes nearest to the ideal when it has fewest laws. In Locke this theory appears in the guise of natural rights. A man brings with him into society rights to life, liberty and property, which society must respect and preserve and cannot infringe.[1] 'The commonwealth seems to me to be a society of men constituted only for the procuring, preserving and advancing their own civil interests. Civil interests I call life, liberty, health, and indolency of body; and the possession of outward things, such as money, lands, houses, furniture, and the like.'[2] It is this tendency in Locke which makes him think of constitutional theory as concerned mainly with putting checks on the government, weakening its authority by dividing it and restricting its

1. Allied to this theory of natural rights is Locke's theory of natural law, which he takes over from earlier political philosophers. This is the view that there is an immutable law governing the just relations between man and man, independently of any society or State to which they may belong. This natural law would serve like natural rights as a limitation on the absolute rule of governments, since it would bind all governments, however constituted and whatever other ends they may pursue.

2. *A Letter concerning Toleration* (Works VI, 9). Cf. *Second Treatise*, ch. VII, paras. 85, 87, 94.

sphere in such a way that all modern legislation and taxation would be condemned out of hand. Whether this respect for 'the liberty of the individual' is more than a national prejudice we must ask later, but for the present we must leave it with the feeling that with it we have left the real Locke.

In *Civil Government*, however, a second view emerges, to which the label is 'democracy'—Locke would say 'popular sovereignty'. It is the theory that a country is ideally governed when it is subject to the will of its own people and not to that of any class or individual. When Locke realises that a total absence of law is not a tolerable ideal, he moves on to the natural view that the laws will leave me as free as ever if they are laws I myself pass or approve. I then obey only myself and my bondage is illusory. It is clear, of course, that the individualist and the democratic theories are wholly distinct and mutually contradictory. The contradictions, however, result only in the emergence of a third view of government which may be labelled (abusively) 'paternalism'. On this theory a law is justified when it is for my good—not merely when it protects me from depraved persons nor when it is one which all the inhabitants approve. 'Law in its true notion is not so much the limitation as the direction of a free and intelligent agent to his own proper interest, and prescribes no farther than is for the general good of those under that law: could they be happier without it, the law as a useless thing would of itself vanish; and that ill deserves the name of confinement which hedges us in only from bogs and precipices.'[1] And again when Locke deals with the problem of rotten boroughs and the exercise of prerogative generally we find that 'whatever cannot but be acknowledged to be of advantage to the society and people in general upon just and lasting measures will always, when done, justify itself.'[2] 'The public good is the rule and measure of all lawmaking.'[3] (Here there is still further confusion. Our third label 'paternalism' has to cover both 'my good' and 'the common good', when it is obvious that these are different and potentially contradictory objects—as in the case of a soldier who is 'detailed' for a forlorn hope. This difficulty will emerge again in Rousseau.)

This is a tenable and powerful doctrine which will require in its turn scrutiny and criticism. But it is a different theory both from individualism and from democracy. The three theories may

1. *Second Treatise*, ch. VI, para. 57.
2. Op. cit., ch. XIII, para. 158, and compare ch. XI, para. 135.
3. *A Letter concerning Toleration* (Works, VI, 30).

be seen in all their mutual hostility when it is stated, for instance, that at the present day the very factors which make our constitution democratic are tending to reduce more and more the liberty of the individual and to destroy more and more all considerations of real public interest. Or it is clear that if Locke were asked whether a particular law were good or bad he would have to give three distinct answers. A law to stop the sale of heroin he must condemn because it infringes my personal liberty to do what I like so long as I do not attack my neighbour. He must simultaneously approve of it because it is for my good and the good of the community, keeping us from the 'bogs and precipices' of the drug habit; while his third attitude (that of the democrat) will swing between condemnation and approval according as the popularity of heroin varies among the fifty million subjects of the Queen.

4

ROUSSEAU

We have made easier the transition to Rousseau by eliciting from Locke his three main doctrines. All three are to be found in Rousseau, with the difference that their mutual inconsistency is clearly seen, and that they consequently appear now as stages in a progress which attempts either to leave behind the less adequate theories or reconcile them with their more developed successors.

Rousseau began by worshipping the Noble Savage and the Golden Age. Like Locke, he regarded Society as a 'fall' from a primitive condition of natural goodness and health. The State is one of those artificial devices which corrupt and deface the clean simplicity of Nature's honest purposes. Although, as we shall see, Rousseau's mature thought completely rejected this identification of the natural with the primitive, of virtue with savagery, yet his influence on his contemporaries was probably mainly in the direction of a 'return to nature'. We can see the germs of the romantic movement and hear the voice of Wordsworth when he speaks of 'men like me whose passions have destroyed their original simplicity, who can no longer subsist on plants or acorns, or live without laws and magistrates.'[1] Virtue obviously means freedom from the claims of the State, and to be nourished on nuts and shod with sandals. 'It is under the homespun of the labourer, and not beneath the gilt and tinsel of the courtier, that we should look for strength and vigour of body.'[2] Unlike Locke, however, Rousseau could not continue his political thinking for

1. *Essay on the Origin of Inequality* (Works [Paris, 1826], vol. 1, p. 365).
2. *Essay on the Arts and Science* (Works 1, 9).

ever in this fairyland of myth and metaphor. He also saw, and he was the first to see clearly, that the state of nature and the social contract are not historical facts but logical abstractions, and that the history of primitive peoples is wholly irrelevant to the problem of political obligation. 'The philosophers, who have enquired into the foundations of society, have all felt the necessity of going back to a state of nature, but not one of them has got there. . . . It has not even entered the heads of most of our writers to doubt whether the state of nature ever existed. . . . Let us begin then by laying facts aside as they do not affect the question. The investigations we may enter into, in treating this subject, must not be considered as historical truths, but only as mere conditional and hypothetical reasonings, rather calculated to explain the nature of things than to ascertain their actual origin.'[1] 'It is no light understanding to distinguish properly between what is original and what is artificial in the actual nature of man, or to form a true idea of a state which no longer exists, perhaps never did exist, and probably never will exist, and of which it is, nevertheless, necessary to have true ideas, in order to form a proper judgment of our present state.'[2] Here we see Rousseau fighting his way from the misleading mythology of Nature and Contract, that mythology from which Hobbes had failed to free himself completely.

What is more important for our purpose is that, having found that 'the state of nature' means 'what would be left if we abstract from our present life the contribution made by society', he realised at once that such a state is no ideal to which anyone could wish to return. The social contract is pure gain. 'The position in which they find themselves as a result of the contract is really preferable to that in which they were before. Instead of renunciation, they have made an advantageous exchange; instead of an uncertain and precarious way of living they have got one that is better and more secure; instead of natural independence they have got liberty; instead of the power to harm others, security for themselves; and instead of their strength, which others might overcome, a right which social union makes invincible.'[3] Whatever freedom they lose and whatever risk of life the demands of the State may impose on them, they would lose and risk a hundredfold in the state of nature. People who glorify the state of nature

1. *The Origin of Inequality* (Works I, 241, 242).
2. Ib., Pref. (Works I, 231).
3. *Contrat Social*, Book II, ch. IV. Cf. Book I, ch. VIII.

have succeeded by a very simple device, 'They have transferred to the state of nature ideas which were acquired in society'[1]— such ideas as justice and property—so that they became blind to the fact that 'natural morality' would be non-existent and 'natural independence' a slavery more terrible than any the worst tyrant has ever laid on his weakest victim. Suppose all Social organisation removed; I should then no longer be 'bound' to any society. I should be 'free' to spend all my time hunting and fishing and sleeping and making my clothes and securing my cave. I should equally be 'compelled' to spend all my time in these pursuits, and should thereby lose completely every scrap of the freedom I now value so highly. All this Rousseau saw, and with it the value and therefore the 'naturalness' of civil society. And forthwith the spectres of the Noble Savage and the Golden Age follow the spectres of Adam and Melchizedek off the stage of political theory. In the vigorous phrase of another clear-headed contemporary of Locke who saw through the shallowness of this contrast of natural and artificial, there will be no more attempts by political philosophers to 'fill the country with naked followers of nature enjoying all the privileges of brutality'.[2] Individualism must now find new arguments to fight the 'interferences' it holds in such detestation. They can no longer be dismissed as 'unnatural'.

By the time he wrote his *Contrat Social*, Rousseau had already achieved the advance we have just described; the 'return to nature' satisfied him only when he was writing the typical prize essay of the clever undergraduate. His political theory thereafter reveals him struggling from the second to the third stage, as their mutual conflicts became clear to him. He sees the value of civil society and thinks it can be justified (1) when its activities follow the will of the people and (2) when they are for the public good.

A reaction from the close and dying aristocracy of the French Court and an admiration for republican Rome and the free cantons of Switzerland show up clearly as the dominant factors determining Rousseau's choice of democracy among the forms of government. Not the will of a class or a tyrant but the will of the whole nation should determine the laws; and this will is to be discovered simply by asking the nation to meet together and declare it. Each citizen then moulds the laws of his country. Repre-

---

1. *The Origin of Inequality* (Works I, 241).
2. Berkeley, *Alciphon* II, ad fin. (Works [Ed. Campbell Fraser, Oxford 1901], vol. II, p. 119).

sentative government is a specious form of slavery.[1] Only when
I actively assist in legislation am I really a citizen and genuinely
free; and, since the fewer the citizens are the more weight my
voice has among them, Rousseau would go back to the small
states of antiquity for his ideal. 'The larger the state the less the
liberty.'[2] By 'liberty' here Rousseau obviously means not freedom
from political control but freedom *for* political control, freedom
to determine the course of legislation. Such a direct democracy
is the only legitimate form of government, because only in such
a constitution does each man 'obey himself alone and remain as
free as before.'[3] But since each man governs himself, the State's
domination is illusory, and therefore may be absolute.[4]

Against this naively democratic view many objections are
obvious, and Rousseau was well aware of them. What is the
point of these meetings if they merely register the unanimous
views of the citizens? When all agree, a law is unnecessary. There
is no law in this country against cannibalism. The outcome is
obvious. Sovereignty of the people means sovereignty of the
majority. But this will not justify political obligation. For if I am
in the majority there is no obligation and if I am in the minority
there is no justification. Rousseau's attempt to meet this problem
takes him straight into the third stage of his development.

He says that if I find myself outvoted I must recognise that
I was mistaken.[5] But mistaken about what? I set out to express
my own wishes; it seems unlikely that I should not know what
they are, and still more unlikely that, when I am thus ignorant,
the decision of a majority of those present and voting should
infallibly enlighten me. Rousseau does end by grasping both
these paradoxes, but we must follow his route. His first move is
to say the citizens are called together to vote not each for what
he wishes but each for what all wish. This takes us little further;
for 'all' appears to mean 'all the others', and such mutual aid is
reminiscent of Scilly Isles economics. But it next appears that
I am to vote neither for what I want nor for what I think the others
want, but for the common good. Only then can it be said that
'each individual, as a man, may have a particular will contrary
or dissimilar to the general will which he has as a citizen. His
particular interest may speak to him quite differently from the
common interest.'[6] Rousseau contrasts this 'general will', which
is the will of the whole community directed to its real interest,

1. *C.S.*, III, ch. XV.   2. *C.S.*, III, ch. I.   3. *C.S.*, I, ch. VI.
4. Cf. *C.S.*, II, ch. IV.   5. *C.S.*, IV., ch. II.   6. *C.S.*, I, ch. VII.

with the 'will of all', which is a mere total of selfish and casually coincident wills.[1] Here at last we have a plausible justification of political obligation, that its force is exercised for the common good. Rousseau goes on to draw some corollaries. By definition the general will is infallible,[2] and therefore it by no means follows that every majority vote expresses it. In some cases the majority is well-meaning but misguided. Here the simple democrat in Rousseau is losing ground. 'How can a blind multitude, which often does not know what it wills because it rarely knows what is good for it, carry out for itself so great and difficult an enterprise as a system of legislation? Of itself the people always wills the good, but of itself it by no means always sees it. . . . This makes a legislator necessary.'[3] Yet Rousseau remains enough of a democrat to feel that the legislator is an anomaly—he attempts to limit his work to a single, original system of laws[4]—thus relapsing into the mythological error he had escaped and forgetting that, for a civilised people, legislation is a continuous activity. He also thinks it necessary for the blind multitude to endorse by its votes those measures it is too stupid to devise. He does not see that, if the general will finds expression in laws which are for the common good, that constitution is best which most safely discovers and passes good laws; and it is far from obvious that the direct democracy of mass meetings is the best instrument. He is gradually realising that the problem of the types of constitution is a secondary and a derivative problem in political theory. The need for reconsidering this question becomes more obvious when Rousseau sees that a majority is not merely often blind, but that it is sometimes not even well-meaning. When a State grows weak 'the common interest finds opponents: . . . the general will ceases to be the will of all, and the best advice is not taken without question'. . . . Finally, 'men guided by secret motives no longer give their views as citizens . . . and iniquitous decrees directed solely to private interest get passed under the name of laws'.[5] And this is not an incident of political decay only but an ever-present danger. 'Hence the law of public order in assemblies is not so much to maintain in them the general will as to secure that the question be always put to it and the answer always given by it.'[6] But to trust to those who 'frame the questions' while relieving them of all responsibility by public vote is surely the direct route to

1. *C.S.*, II, ch. III. 2. *C.S.*, II, ch. III. 3. *C.S.*, II, ch. VI.
4. *C.S.*, II, ch. VII. 5. *C.S.*, IV, ch. I. 6. Ib.

demagogy, and Rousseau in at least one place gives up altogether
the mass-meeting and its political activity. 'But how, I shall be
asked, can the general will be known in cases in which it has not
expressed itself? Must the whole nation be assembled together
at every unforeseen event? Certainly not. It ought the less to be
assembled because it is by no means certain that its decision would
be the expression of the general will; besides, the method
would be impracticable in a great people, and is hardly ever necessary where the government is well-intentioned: for the rulers
well know that the general will is always on the side which is
most favourable to the public interest, that is to say most equit-
able; so that it is needful only to act justly, to be certain of following the general will.'[1] Here the active vote of the people has
dropped from being the sole source of real law to the mere
negative position of a safeguard to be invoked when the government 'flout equity too openly'. Elsewhere too we find the significant admission that 'what makes the will general is less the
numbers of voters than the common interest uniting them.'[2]
Here we have moved far from 'the larger the State the less the
liberty'.

Rousseau has a further step to take before his vindication of
law is complete. Law is an expression of the general will, which is
the will of a society for the common good. It therefore demands
my respect. But the common good is also my good; and so, finally,
in obeying the law I am pursuing my own best interests and
achieving what I really will, despite the opposition of passing
and irrational desires. 'When in the popular assembly a law is
proposed, what the people is asked is not exactly whether it
approves or rejects the proposal, but whether it is in conformity
with the general will, which is their will.'[3] 'It is to law alone that
men owe justice and liberty. . . . It is the celestial voice which
dictates to each citizen the precepts of public reason, and teaches
him to act according to the rules of his own judgment, and not to
behave inconsistently with himself.'[4] And so we reach the famous
paradox 'This means nothing less than that he will be forced to
be free.'[5] The final position is just that improbability from which
we turned aside. I may not know what I really want and a majority
may enlighten me.

1. *Discourse on Political Economy* (Works I, 424).   2. *C.S.*, II, ch. IV.
3. *C.S.*, IV, ch. II.   4. *Discourse on Political Economy* (Works I, 420).
5. *C.S.*, I, ch. VII.

5

HEGEL AND THE HEGELIANS

We reached with Rousseau the paradox that a good law is wrongly conceived as restricting liberty, that it forces me to be free. Such a law in promoting the good of my community achieves something which I actually will. It is true that at the moment I may desire other objects more, but then I am reminded that the common good is not only something I do desire but something I ought to promote. The law thus reinforces an element in my nature and one which I rank higher than others. Law is therefore both 'natural' and 'moral'.

I am asking the reader, then, to select a law which he would agree is in the public interest. I might suggest the law against blackmail or that controlling the sale of poisons or one of the less controversial sections of the road traffic legislation. If he applies Rousseau's analysis in such a case the force of his position will be clear. Even if I want to blackmail or to take cocaine or to drive all over the road in defiance of the traffic signals, I also desire the general objects which the laws in question promote —peace, health, and security; and though for the moment I desire them less, I ought to (and in a calm hour I shall) desire them more. Therefore when the law (by removal of opportunity or threat of punishment) enters the arena it sides with and makes explicit and permanent my unreliable and intermittent will to good. It is no more tyrannical than my doctor who says 'you must drop potatoes' or my tailor who says 'you must have an extra row of braid'.

The force and vigour of this doctrine as it developed from

B

Rousseau soon carried it to further triumphs. Where the State had once been shown to be not only a natural but a liberating and a moralising institution, it was made by Hegel and his followers to absorb into itself the whole of freedom and morality.

This movement we shall now follow, making it as clear and as plausible as possible and leaving all misgivings and qualifications to a later stage. We shall trace the dialectic by which all authority and all objectives other than the State and its needs are shown to be inadequate to satisfy a human personality and to render morality a reasonable system. The whole movement can be summed up as the self-development of the concept of freedom.

The dialectic of desire. (*a*) We think of freedom first as abstract or absolute. Obviously, we say, the will must be free to choose its object no matter what its desires may be and without relation to their relative strength and attractiveness. For without that freedom I am irresponsible. The act of choice must be itself unmotived. Nothing shall influence or affect it. Here we have erected into an ideal the emptiest condition we can imagine. It is a condition in which no will can actually stand for a moment, without annihilation, and yet one to which in certain phases of dissatisfaction with self or environment we are all alike attracted. We then feel any definite object or activity as a chain. Anarchy for anarchy's sake, asceticism as an end in itself, the everlasting Nay —these are the nearest titles we can discover for a condition which (could anyone but achieve it) would find even in any particular desire of its own a restriction, even in an institution set up by itself a tyrant. It is an ideal which is destructive because it is wholly negative, impotent because necessarily indefinite.

(*b*) Now this attitude is clearly an ideal limit, which no continuing life could maintain, and it swings at once into its opposite. The will, then, instead of finding all desires bad and hostile, is identified with any and all as they come to hand. In the first stage to be free meant to be free *from* anything whatever; now it means to be free *for* anything whatever. Liberty is now the capacity to achieve whatever at any moment I desire. The prior stage we labelled 'ascetic' in its attitude to impulse, this we may label 'naturalist'. It is the will of caprice and chance and like the first is a practical impossibility and a mere ideal limit. For the slightest trace of rational planning or definite policy is treachery to its principle, because a continuing policy means momentary sacrifices, and a plan for the future would force on caprice a stability which it must reject as servitude. As with all triads, the first stage was blank identity, the second sheer diversity. The first preserved the self by making action impossible, the second saves action by destroying the self.

(c) The solution of this dilemma—either impotence or caprice, either an empty self or a chain of isolated impulses—can be found only if both demands are satisfied, and this can occur only when the self and the impulses are alike seen to be abstractions, when the desires are recognised as phases of will in a rational system which is the self—or (if this is to rush ahead too quickly) when they are so reflected on and understood that each can be accepted as expressing a reasonable need of the self as a whole and as therefore requiring a satisfaction to which its mere existence or strength alone woud not entitle it. Here was the force of Aristotle's recognition that the desires are neither good nor bad and that desire made one with that practical wisdom which 'is in a sense the whole of virtue' is the keynote of right action. Freedom now is re-defined and becomes the capacity to satisfy a desire not merely because it happens to be present and overpowering in strength (to such desires as that we often and rightly call ourselves slaves), but when it is such that I can throw my whole heart into its satisfaction. 'I move in the desire, it does not move me.' This synthesis of self and desire may be achieved below the level of explicit and systematic self-consciousness. A child's resistance to interference is the measure more often of the power of the thwarted personality than of the strength of its desire for the particular object it is pursuing. Plato spoke of this rightly as something different from desire and more rational in its nature, though he made the mistake of treating it as a part of the soul; and analytic psychology having determined to dissect the soul into instincts is often compelled to add to its list a monstrosity named 'the instinct of self-assertion', which is really not a fourteenth instinct but the whole self forcing its way back into the arena inhabited by the thirteen already introduced.[1]

The dialectic of the object. (a) The conclusion of our last triad led easily to the assumption that objects which could satisfy the whole self must have some common character or product for the

---

1. Cf. for example McDougall, *Social Psychology*, p. 62, with his definition of an instinct (p. 29) as 'a disposition which determines its possessor to perceive and to pay attention to objects of a certain class, to experience an emotional excitement of a particular quality on perceiving such an object, and to act in regard to it in a particular manner'. What is the particular object and the specific reaction of the instinct of self-assertion?

sake of which each of them was desired. If such a common character is sought it can be found only in pleasantness. It was assumed that because it was the same self which always felt the desire it must always desire the same thing. How else could two objects be compared or a rational choice justified? Here again, as the first member of a new triad, is the inevitable abstract identity which detaches our view from all the differences between objects and demands that if they are to be related at all they can be related only by the homogeneity of qualitative identity.

(b) Butler exposed the weakness of this hedonistic psychology by recalling it to the obvious facts. Pleasure is in general the accompaniment of successful action, of action which achieves its object. Pleasure may also be itself an object; activities or objects may be desired for the pleasure they produce. But in the vast majority of our actions, some end other than pleasure is desired, and pleasure ensues, if it ensues at all, as an unforeseen bonus. For one example of this, the following quotation[1] is of interest. 'Climbing for its own sake is and always has been the chief motive in mountaineering. . . . It has many pleasures of its own, but, above all, the climber is possessed by such climbing far more strongly than he can ever be held by a view or by the contemplation of his own thoughts and feelings, should that be his habit . . . the action wholly absorbs his attention; and he knows it would do so, even if it gave no mental or physical pleasure by itself.' There is all the difference in the world between eating a square meal and eating sweets. 'Desire terminates on its object' and hunger is a desire for food and not a desire for pleasure. Here is the inevitable reaction from abstract identity to sheer particularity. Hedonism held that all desires were one single desire, the desire for pleasure, a desire for a state of the self and the same state of the self. Now Butler throws the object entirely outside the self, and it becomes a plurality of separate externals.[2]

(c) It remains as before to complete the movement by meeting the claims of both sides. Butler's view that particular desires are 'movements towards somewhat external' is certainly truer than Bentham's that 'the motive in prospect is always some pleasure or some pain'. Yet Butler is also inaccurate. These external ob-

---

1. *Brenva*, T. Graham Brown, p. xiii.
2. Butler, *Sermons*, Preface para. 35 and Sermon II para 13 (Ed. Bernard) —Selby Bigge, *British Moralists*, vol. I, paras. 198, 218; and cf. Plato's analysis of thirst. (Rep. IV, 437 d.)

jects, food, drink, money, which I am said to desire, are existent when and before I desire them. What I desire is not *them*, their existence—but some activity *of my own* in which they are involved. My object is 'the eating of the food, the possession of the money'. A child who cries for the moon is not consoled by the assurance that there *is* the moon. It desires the moon to have and to hold and to suck also. Desire, then, on further analysis, is seen to be desire for a state of affairs involving *both* the external object with its real difference from other objects *and* the reference to the single self.[1]

We may turn aside here to examine in some detail an attempt to arrest the movement of the dialectic at this point and to maintain that the good at which I aim will always be the satisfaction of myself. We shall examine the theory in T. H. Green because it is explicitly defended by him. Hegel is obscure on this point and Bradley's treatment is itself so thoroughly dialectical that we cannot assert that 'self-realisation' means for him the realisation of *my* self in any sense which can distinguish *my* self from God or from the United Kingdom of Great Britain and Northern Ireland. Bosanquet indeed commits himself to Green's position but only as an afterthought where he is meeting objections.[2] We shall find that 'self-realisation', or the satisfaction of the finite self, breaks down as certainly as hedonism if it is taken as a definition of the good, unless 'self' is widened in a way which Green's own theory forbids.

We must certainly agree with Green in his analysis of hunger, thirst or miserliness that each is a desire not merely for an external object but for a state of affairs in which my self (eating, drinking, possessing) is involved. But Green passes on to the general position that every desire I have is a desire for a state of affairs which involves the satisfaction of myself. Self-satisfaction is the form of all action; even the martyr seeks his own satisfaction through pain or sacrifice. 'Anything conceived as good in such a way that the agent acts for the sake of it must be conceived as *his own* good.'[3] Now this seems as clearly false as the previous contentions were clearly true. Green at once admits that only if the martyr attained to the consciousness of the completion of his work would he gain the satisfaction which is said to be his

1. T. H. Green, *Prolegomena to Ethics*, paras. 86, 131. I have altered 'acquisition' of money to 'possession' for reasons defended below (p. 43).
2. *Philosophical Theory of the State*, pp. 291, 292.
3. *Prolegomena to Ethics*, para. 92 and cf. paras. 91, 159.

object. But surely he may know that he will not live to see the completion, and then it will be clear that the completion (which can occur) and not the satisfaction (which cannot) is the object he desires. If we look to an example which does not raise the additional question of self-identification with a church or cause (discussed below[1]) we may find it when a miser leaves his fortune to charity in order to annoy his relatives. His aim is their annoyance, and though he (like the martyr) may achieve various incidental satisfactions of his own none of these is his object.[2] Self-satisfaction then is not 'the form of all action' and there appear to be states of affairs whose occurrence is desired and which do not involve or contain as an essential element the agent's own satisfaction.

The dialectic of other selves. In the previous stages of the dialectic 'externality' has meant merely the externality of the physical world which I use and use rightly, as a mere means to the satisfaction of my self. But with the appearance of other selves a new problem arises. In this section we shall treat it as far as possible at a level below that of explicit morality, though the line is hard to maintain at all consistently.

(*a*) Here again the obvious 'first-glance' conception of freedom is that of freedom *from* others, the claim to live my own life unaffected by those around me. Could such a freedom be maintained, it would be mere animal savagery. We think of Robinson Crusoe, but we forget that he landed on his island with the influences of a hundred million men and five thousand years of social life stamped on him. Deprive him of the wheel, the lever, the alphabet, and his story would be a very different one. We took as the model of our isolated individual the hermit with his freedom from interference, but his freedom is illusory. Forces act on him and mould him even if they are only the mute forces of the walls of his cell. An alternative individualism which offers more hope lies open. Instead of cutting himself off from all external influences a man may plunge into the arena determined to retain his individuality by open warfare. He will still regard all personal contacts as 'ties' or fetters on his sacrosanct independence; and other wills appear to him as mere force and necessity to be beaten down or used for his private ends. Men are merely rivals, customers, or 'hands', to be crushed or outwitted or enslaved. His highest achievement apart from the joy of the actual conflict

1. P. 40.
2. See further below for exposure of possible confusions here (pp. 39–41).

can only be material comfort. His isolation is spiritually as complete as the hermit's and no more satisfying.[1]

(b) The reaction from this ideal is found in the undiscriminating philanthropist. His attitude to others is universal sympathy. He is egalitarian, cosmopolitan, benevolent by impulse and with caprice. He is correspondingly impotent. If he does good it will be by chance; if he does harm he will have the same glow of satisfaction and claim the same approval.

(c) Once again we require our synthesis, a service of others but a service justified by my status in regard to them, and made rational, coherent, purposive and effective by being the service of a society to which both they and I belong. In defending the synthesis against the second member of the triad, Hegel is fighting, as often, against much of our popular and cherished belief. We naturally think that the wider a man's sympathies the better his action, and that 'humanitarian' is one of the world's noblest titles. But it is not the width of the sympathy which Hegel is attacking, but its unorganised particularity. The devotion of a research scientist to the relief of cancer is as good a specimen of the synthesis as the devotion of a patriot to his country. For it is the attachment of the feeling to a specific cause and its concentration in continuous and effective work, in contrast with its scattering in isolated sporadic acts of benevolent impulse, which is the demand of this synthesis. The members of this triad (Ishmael, Kim and Jonathan, if you like) are still to be thought of as under non-moral impulse, and the synthesis, though necessarily an advance on its antithesis, is not yet an advance into morality.

It is obvious that one of the most general and primitive forms of this final attitude to others is found in family affection and the actions it inspires. Here again Green's view that action is always directed to the satisfaction of the self meets with further difficulties. When a man desires to bring about the good of his children he is said to be aiming, as he always must, at a better state of himself,[2] though in this case he identifies his good with the good of others. 'The well-being of a family with which he identifies himself

1. The story 'A Stoic' in Galsworthy's *Five Tales* gives an excellent picture of the type at its best and most successful. Heythorp's fellow directors are to be 'bear-led', his shareholders to be 'diddled'. His daughter is a 'tie' on him. His creed and his last word of advice are 'There is only one thing in life that matters—independence.' His only recognition of society is shown in capricious charity to his illegitimate children.

2. Op. cit., para. 190.

and of which the continuity is as his own possesses his mind.'[1]
Now suppose the action dictated by this affection is to provide
for his family by making a will or insuring his life, how can we
hold that the man's aim is a better state of himself? No doubt the
welfare of his children would satisfy him if he lived to see it, but
the conditions of our example preclude his doing so, therefore
this satisfaction cannot be his object. No doubt also the contemplation of their future welfare gives him satisfaction, but this
cannot be the satisfaction he desires to bring about, for he
enjoys it before he acts at all. No doubt the actual signing of the
will or paying of the premium may give him some satisfaction
and improve his character, but this again cannot be the satisfaction or the better state which he desires to produce, for he
would have produced both, even if the will were immediately
burnt or the insurance company collapsed the next morning;
and in such a case he would certainly say his object had not been
achieved. Therefore none of these incidental satisfactions (however undeniable their existence) can be that *good for him* at which
he is said to aim.

Are we to postulate an immortality for him to contain the
satisfaction required? 'Everyone immortalises himself who looks
forward to realisation of ideal objects . . . objects in which he
thinks of himself as still living when dead.'[2] Obviously the satisfaction cannot be placed in the cruder form of private immortality
with its private enjoyment, for this would necessitate that only
believers in personal immortality would be good parents or
citizens. The immortality required must be of that figurative kind
which makes Shakespeare live on in his work and finds Euclid
active for good and for evil in our schools. We must take seriously
that 'identification of himself with his family' quoted above. Now
it is true that some philosophers have found a self-realisation view
tenable, in the face of the obvious difficulties we have just raised,
by thus widening the conception of 'self', and the consideration
of their views will form part of a later discussion.[3] But for Green
this route is closed, for he is emphatic that it is *my* self which is
to be satisfied, and also that 'wider selves' such as a 'national
self' are fictions. The so-called national self is simply 'the persons
who compose the nation as modified by their intercourse with
each other'.[4] It seems to me false on introspection that a man
identifies his own self with that of his family or those of his

1. Ib., para. 229.   2. Op. cit., para. 229.
3. See below, p. 141.   4. Op. cit., para. 184.

children, or his good with their good; but, even if he did so, on Green's own showing he would be merely making a mistake and becoming the victim of an illusion. Action performed under such an impulse would be self-defeating and impossible to an intelligent person who had reflected on the privacy of selfhood.

We might reach the same conclusion by turning against Green one of his own arguments against Hedonism. He is pleading against the confusions of Mill in his transition from 'my pleasure' to 'the pleasure of the greatest number', and he says: 'To be actuated by a desire for pleasure is to be actuated by a desire for some specific pleasure to be enjoyed by oneself. No two persons whose desires were only of this kind could really desire anything in common.'[1] If satisfaction may be distinguished from pleasure it seems obvious that the same arguments apply. Satisfaction may come to me after a strenuous climb or a long afternoon's digging in the garden, but it comes unsought for the most part. If my strenuous climb is forced on me by my missing the last funicular, I may buoy myself up with an *olim meminisse iuvabit*, but the aim of the mountaineer who is self-determined and not train-determined is not this subsequent glow, even though he knows it may await him with his slippers at his inn. If we recognise that we cannot share satisfaction with others in any literal sense, how are we to avoid making them merely means to our own?[2] How can I treat others as ends and yet believe that the only end for me is a better state of myself? Occasionally we feel Green has simply lost sight of the problem through a confusion of terms (like that which enables Pragmatism to call itself 'Humanism' instead of 'Egoism'). When, for instance, he says, 'Contribution to *human* perfection is the object in which he seeks satisfaction',[3] or 'The goodness of *men* lies in devotion to the ideal of *humanity*',[4] the danger is apparent. But elsewhere he is clear enough that my own perfection is my only possible object.[5] Now if we are unable to identify my self with other selves, what relation is there to be between them? I am to 'aim at a good conceived as *shared* by others'.[6] I am to seek 'a well-being in which the permanent well-being of others is *included*'.[7]

But the only good at which I can aim is perfection of my self, and that cannot include but only accompany the perfection of

1. Ib., p. 161, para. 282.
2. Op. cit., para. 190.
3. Ib., para. 191 (italics mine throughout).
4. Ib., para. 196.
5. E.g. paras. 181, 183, 195.
6. Para. 199.
7. Para. 201.

others, nor can they share my perfection. And, finally, when a community is said to be founded on 'a unity of self-consciousness' the most casual reader must notice the contradiction between such a phrase and Green's insistence on the essential privacy of self-consciousness. If others cannot share my satisfaction or well-being it still seems inadequate to say that their well-being should merely accompany mine, as Green must-if he is to be consistent. 'The idea of a perfect self-conscious life for myself will involve the idea of a perfection of all other beings, *so far as* I find the thought of their being perfect necessary to my self-satisfaction.'[1] But surely the truth is that a mother pursues the good of her children neither as a means to her own self-satisfaction nor just 'so far as' she finds the thought of their well-being essential to it. Their good is an essential element (and essential just because it is theirs and not hers) in what she is trying to produce. Green is on firmer ground when he says, 'Except as between persons each recognising the other as an end in himself and having the will to treat him as such, there can be no society.'[2] The real doubt is whether my own well-being is always or ever essential to my aim .in such a case. It may ensue on my action or be realised in it, but that (as with pleasure) is another story.

What we have seen in Green (and this is the reason why we have devoted so much space to him) is the dialectic actually in operation breaking down the most enlightened and pertinacious self-realisation theory in the direction of a genuine common good. We may add three quotations showing stages in this liberation. Morality begins with social good: 'what is good for man as a member of a community'.[3] 'The distinction of good for self and good for others has never entered into that idea of a true good on which moral judgments are founded.'[4] A man's power of contemplating the perfectibility of himself is 'in promise and potency an interest in the bettering of mankind . . . conceived as an absolutely desirable end'.[5] In these sentences we see the idea of my own perfection first connected with, then submerged in, and finally subordinated to, the idea of the good of others.

There is one last remedy by which Green attempts to escape from the necessity of a trans-subjective goal of action. We recall that 'the eating of food' and not 'food' alone is what I really desire when I am hungry. So now when it is suggested that the good of others or some better way of communal living is my

1. Para. 370.   2. Para. 190.   3. Para. 232.
4. Para. 232.   5. Para. 240.

object in altruistic action, Green restates these aims as 'the *production* of the good of others' or 'the *establishment* of a way of life'. Now the good of others may not be my good nor their way of life my life (since I may die before either is achieved), but the production and the establishment, at which I am said to aim, will yet be mine. So my aim is something that is *mine* after all. For the good citizen, 'the thought of his well-being will be to him the thought of himself as living in *the successful pursuits* of various interests which the order of society has determined for him, interests ranging from *provision* for his family to the *improvement* of the public health or the *production* of a system of philosophy'.[1] This, however, will not save him, for the production, provision, etc., are not the goals of actions but the actions themselves. There also then the good at which my act is aimed is not a state of me. It was a similar slip which makes Green say that 'the *acquisition* of treasure' is the object on which the miser's heart is set.[2] Philip Armour, the American millionaire, was asked by a journalist why he did not retire. He replied: 'I do not want any more money. I do not love the money; what I do love is the getting of it, the making it.' *His* heart was set on the acquisition of wealth, but just for that reason he was no miser. For the miser, acquisition is the act; but possession is the object of the act.

So we may return to the main line of our argument with the certainty that the synthesis of the last triad should be desire for the good of others who are related to me in some determinate way such that I have the right and the duty and the capacity to promote their good. We shall remember to admit that, when my act has this aim, besides the good it produces, there comes into existence its own intrinsic goodness as being an act consciously so aimed. But we shall feel also that this intrinsic goodness need not and cannot be the aim of my act even in part or incidentally. We may well believe that the paradox of pleasure is true here too, that if I aim at self-improvement or satisfaction I am likely to miss them, and even perhaps that, except as derivative from and a means to the good of others, there is no duty of self-improvement at all.

The dialectic of duty. Throughout the last section we found it difficult to avoid crossing from action to moral action both because Green finds the roots of morality in family affection and also because of the deeply ingrained tendency to identify selfishness with immorality and morality with altruism. Popular ethics

---

1. Para. 234 (italics mine).   2. Para. 86.

have not yet assimilated Butler's distinction between actions arising from self-love and those arising from particular propensions. Nor have they seen that many of the actions thought to be moral or altruistic really arise from particular propensions. A mother's defence of her children, a stateman's promotion of his country's interests, may be the expressions of impulses as natural or instinctive or non-moral as hunger or thirst. 'If eating and drinking be natural, herding is so too.'[1] Nepotism and patriotism may be foes of the good as potent as gluttony or avarice.

We now come to deal explicitly with actions which a man does not because he wants to do them but because he thinks he ought to. The ground here is familiar to every student of ethics and traversed in every text-book, so we can afford to be even more wantonly brief and dogmatic than in the previous sections.[2]

When once the growing mind frees itself from the tutelage of some *de facto* authority and demands a basis for its morality, it meets with instant difficulty. Unreflective duty can take its imperative from the dooms of Zeus, from priest or parent, from the custom of tribe or city, and act in peace and faith. But the first conflict unveils an Antigone and the question 'Whose standard?' soon brings down all standards. Conscience, it seems, must create its own imperatives, yet demand a place in the objective order of events which it challenges. The world sets its problems and accepts its solutions, yet its quest seems to be an inner one, 'searching the heart'. Sometimes it firmly asserts the dominance of the inner voice. I may reject the world as it comes to me from the past and say, 'I know I made that promise, incurred those debts, that I have received help and myself given pledges to fortune, yet I feel I should neglect them all and follow my revelation of duty'; or when it challenges me for the future I may reject it equally. 'I know my action will create ill-feeling and foster misery; I know that my friends will despise me, and that the cause for which I act is already lost, so that the only people to benefit from what I do will be those vultures which hover on the horizons of failure; yet I feel I ought to do it, and "mere externals" cannot count against the conviction of duty.' In such situations the paradox is plain. It is not mere private feeling which can thus plunge an external order into chaos. For the order it assails is no 'external order' after all. My friends and my family are not ex-

1. Shaftesbury.
2. Cf. Hegel, *Rechtsphilosophie*, paras. 133–4 (and Reyburn, *The Ethical Theory of Hegel*, pp. 59–62, 173–5, for an excellent summary and exposition).

ternal accidents and their claims are forces as much part of myself as part of the world. My creditors and my countrymen are such *only* because I have a self which is capable of honesty and loyalty. So when I stand on a 'feeling of duty' against these 'outer claims' I am not merely setting myself against the world, but a single impulse of myself against all the rest of it, against its friendship and honour and loyalty and love. This conflict of 'external' and 'internal' in the moral field the dialectic next attempts to remove.

(*a*) Kant's central merit is his insistence on the ethical priority and absoluteness of the concept of duty. But, as every critic has pointed out, the command 'Do your duty, because it is your duty' does not tell me what my duty is. Kant's empty form of duty is therefore naturally the first member of a moral triad— the blank identity as usual divorced from all detail and standing as a mere common factor over against the specific duties it ought to determine and relate.

(*b*) The natural reaction of the plain man to this criticism of Kant is that everyone knows what in any particular set of circumstances his duty is, and even if he did not it is no part of the task of ethical theory to tell him. But it is the task of ethical theory to discover whether definite types of action are considered to be duties, and what reasons, if any, people would give for believing specific acts to be duties, and what reasons, even if they would give none, there actually are. Against such questions the plain man's simple belief develops into an explicit moral theory, the theory of intuitionism. It holds that I know my duty in each particular case and that I can give no reasons, nor are there any, why I should assert this act or that to be my duty, except the self-evidence of every particular instance. Nor are there 'sorts of actions' which are duties, in the sense that recognition of the 'sort' is required prior to recognition of the particular duty. The 'sorts' if they exist at all are classes empirically determined, after the particular recognition of duty, by the discovery of similarities in the particular cases. This theory is the natural second member of our triad, the plunge into sheer particularity, the field, as ever, of caprice and chaos and unrelated difference. Neither Kant nor the Intuitionist (since both consider moral action in abstraction from the kind of end pursued) can allow errors of moral judgment. A life of conscientious self-devotion which is self-defeating—a life devoted to the dissemination of a degrading superstition or the satisfaction of a barbaric code of revenge—is as good as a life given to the relief of suffering or to the destruction of such codes or superstitions.

(c) It is a sufficient reply to the Intuitionist to point out that we do sometimes give ourselves reasons why we think we ought to do certain acts. We do not first see the act (as this act, in isolation) to be the right act now for us, and later 'classify' it as contributory to health or peace. The reverse is the case. Unless we had seen it did so contribute and had believed that health or peace were good, we should never have thought the act a duty at all. There is no more obviously false doctrine in morals than that which holds that moral rules are empirical generalisations from observed particulars. Their status is indeed odd and puzzling; but, whatever it is, it is not that. The synthesis which we now reach is that this derivation of rightness of acts from the social good they produce is *everywhere* applicable. The common good is the ultimate object of moral endeavour. Here is the filling for Kant's empty concept of duty, here the objective standard which intuitionism refused to allow. Here is a unity of end with a diversity of means, and the reconciliation of form with content.

If we ask why, in many cases, we do not trace the good produced in order to judge the act right, or again how we are able to act at all when every choice would seem to require omniscience in the chooser, the answer is threefold. Firstly, the common good is nearly always at our doors. We need not survey mankind from China to Peru when there is illness in our own household or suffering down the street. Institutions like the family, the Church, the trade union, the village, concentrate and rationalise the dutiful will so that it may have a cutting edge where there is most weight for good behind its blade. Secondly, beneficent laws and institutions are the background of our education and become second nature in our moral life, so that we need not re-think on every occasion the question of their merits. Thirdly, more good is often done by the regularity of a system than by the calculation of good in each several instance.

Indeed the good of a number of persons can sometimes be achieved only by the creation of institutions and laws, and Hegel for the most part refers rather to this social structure as the source of duties than to the ultimate good the structure must subserve. This over-emphasis is due in part to his horror of the excesses of the revolutionary spirit whose empty humanitarianism would abolish even the institutions the people themselves had set up, in its determination to pursue the good unfettered by any specific instruments for the purpose.[1] It is the same spirit which supposes that the common good can be dissociated from law and government and which holds marriage an insult to love,[2] or a creed a fetter on religious experience.[3]

As a result of the dialectic we have been driven to the conclusion that nothing will satisfy either the needs of a conscious subject or the claims of the moral imperative except the service of a common good. It must be admitted that against all the stages we have passed on the way (asceticism, naturalism, hedonism, intuitionism) its claim to supersede and transcend them is more than made out. We must add that, whatever criticism may emerge, this is the only convincing *single* answer to the questions 'What will satisfy a human self?' and 'What is the chief end of man?' The alternative, as we shall discover, is a frank and explicit pluralism of moral values—a pluralism to be unified only by an appeal beyond philosophy to faith or mysticism.

The position we have reached, then, is that every act which is right and satisfying to a human agent is so because it serves to bring about a social or common good.

During the preceding argument we have obviously made a complete change in the meaning of political obligation, a transition from the obligation to obey law and government to that wider obligation which may constrain a citizen in his whole moral life as well as in his abstentions from crime or rebellion. This transition can now be made more explicit and more fully defended. We are asking in this book about the power of the State over her citizens. The first answer is the power of law with the sanction of force.

But there is a vaguer power, that of custom or convention of ethical use-and-wont, which is no less real and insistent. Who makes me observe good manners? The question is ill-put. There is a code of manners which is peculiarly a national code; and it has no sanction but 'public opinion', and that is seldom an effective sanction. Yet the sanction is rendered the less necessary by the fact that to most of us this code is so much part of our nature that it does not seem 'external' at all. We regard the act of giving up a seat in a train to an old woman not as our enslavement to an independent authority but as the 'self-expres-

1. Hegel, *Rechtsphilosophie*, para. 5 add.
2. On marriage as the really true *free* love, paras. 162–6. Here our triad may be Diogenes, Don Juan, Darby and Joan.
3. Cf. para. 141.

sion' of an ordinary decent person; and unless we have considered
the matter we are liable to find in the actions of citizens of other
countries (in their rudeness to servants or their punctual arrival
at the opera) not an equal slavery to another code, but the rather
pitiable vagaries of people who do not know how to behave.
Then we pity the servants (who would be horrified at any greater
familiarity) or show surprise when our own 'English' arrival at
the opera is met with enmity by those whom we disturb, or the
more explicit hostility of closed doors and the loss of Act I.

It is obvious that this code demands from the citizens much
more than law could ever enforce, though we may see occasional
interactions of the two codes, when a policeman keeps his eye
on a queue, or a magistrate verbally castigates an offender he is
powerless to punish.

This is not all. The State requires us to be not merely law-
abiding and decently courteous; it demands service. In the transition from law to convention we saw how the outward could
become inward, how the sanction of force was replaced by the
more elusive powers of education and imitation, so that the complete slave to convention can feel more certain than anyone that
his actions are properly and genuinely self-originated. It is only
a fly small enough and sedentary enough to be carried along on
the axle that can rejoice in the delusion that it is raising a dust.
It may be said that many men do in fact follow their private
consciences in disregard of conventional demands on them, and
yet their moral lives are not empty or capricious, but have an
apparent consistency and stability and an enviable firmness of
tissue which a Hamlet, so intensely aware of the complexity of
the claims on him as to be impotent, would seem grievously to
lack. But these strong and solid consciences usually turn out, on
enquiry, to originate in some institution whose code the man has
so completely assimilated that he has forgotten its source entirely.
In these social contacts of his buried past lies the origin of his
rebel conscience. When he refuses to follow the crowd and stamp
on a man who is down because it is 'not cricket', he is really still
marching with the crowd of his preparatory school, whose names
are lost to him, but whose imperatives, once external to him and
resisted by his every effort, are now the complete furniture of his
moral code. When he refuses to follow England into war, it is
because he has followed the Society of Friends into peace. Thus
the social order creates its rebels as well as its servants and the
'individual conscience' still eludes our search. A man who has

never considered this in his own case can often see it clearly in his friends. 'It never troubles him that mere accident has decided which of those numerous worlds' (i.e. sects, parties, classes) 'is the object of his reliance, and that the same causes which make him a Churchman in London would make him a Buddhist or a Confusian in Pekin.'[1] Or again, the man who says 'I may not know what is good but I know what I like' may seem to be fleeing from an objective order into the recesses of his own self. Yet when he tells you *what* he likes you will see not him but his caste or class or school.

This loss of individuality inevitable under law and convention is made good by the conception of service. There is no reason why service of a community should not be sufficiently Protean to meet the needs of any individual idiosyncrasy of gifts or character; and in most striking cases it is just the fact that no one else can render to the State the service he can which renders its claim paramount on the individual. For examples we may think of the demand made on Lord Kitchener in 1914 or on Mr Churchill in 1940. Or, if we prefer the decent obscurity of a learned language, we may turn to Cincinnatus.

Law, convention, service: these are the demands society makes on its members. But there is a further power which the State can exercise, and without which no civilised State could survive. We may approach it through a parallel. I may occasionally meet an Oxford college tutor to whom the college is everything. His public lectures are dull; he writes no books; he holds no university office; he has no 'outside interest'. But he knows all the members of the college, is constantly consulted by them, follows their achievements in later life and wears every college success like a feather in his own cap. Every moment of his life and every ambition he has is identified with the college. Now when a foreigner comes to Oxford and asks me about the colleges and their powers over their members, I show him first the 'college rules', which compel early rising and prohibit matutinal gramophones. (This is parallel to the sphere of law.) Then I show him the college hall and tell him how convention has allotted a certain table at dinner to persons of special distinction. No rule keeps men away from it and promotion to it is conferred by tacit consent. (This is the power of custom.) Then I add that if he went about among the men he would probably discover a general opinion that everybody should 'do something for the college'; still vaguer this and

1. Mill, *On Liberty*, ch. II (Everyman Edition, p. 80).

more easily evaded, and probably limited to games, but by no means negligible. (This is the conception of service in however narrow and misguided a form.) But I should not feel I had shown my stranger the full power of the college system unless I had let him talk for a little to the college tutor I described above. This is the power a college *can* have over its members, and I should be tempted to add that without him and his like the college system would have a short life indeed.

So, in considering the powers of the State, we must mention law, custom and service, but we must not forget to bring forward, in evidence of a greater power still, such men as Burke or Grey or Haldane or Mazzini. We talk of 'State machinery' and the red tape which wreathes Whitehall; but men do not give up a private practice worth a small fortune for red tape alone, nor give their prime to unremitting labour and their later years to uncomplaining obloquy for a machine. If you say it is desire for power and publicity, I shall quote a statesman who disliked publicity as much as he loved birds and the country. 'I am not going to give you instruction about birds. Like many people who have been at the mercy of public life, which is a very tyrannical affair, I have passed the age of sixty and still have such a deficiency of information that I am not really capable of giving instruction about anything.'[1] No doubt he would not have had his life otherwise, but that confirms my point; and, if it requires further enforcement, there are two letters to Cobden[2] which show how the service of the State can crush private interest and feeling. Bright says: '*Personally*, I would wish to have no meeting, but personally I would not be in public life. I would rather see more after my own interests and the interests of my children. But we are on the rails and must move on. We have work and must do it.'[3] Peel writes, 'You will believe . . . that office and power may be anything but an object of ambition, and that I must be insane if I could be induced by anything but a sense of public duty to undertake what I have undertaken this session.'[4] We have asked what a State is, and the answer will depend on the citizen. To the criminal it may well be a tyrant, and to the plain citizen it often no doubt dons red tape and clanks like a machine. But to such men as Peel and Bright their country has another guise. Again the difference can be illustrated only by quotations which will teach nothing

1. Lord Grey, *Falloden Papers*.
2. Quoted by G. Wallas, *The Great Society*, pp. 146, 159.
3. Bright to Cobden, Jan. 1853.   4. Peel to Cobden, June, 1846.

alike to those who know and to those who do not. 'When I ask myself what I mean by England, when I think of England when I am abroad, England comes to me through my various senses—through the ear, through the eye, and through certain imperishable scents. . . . The sounds of England, the tinkle of the hammer on the anvil in the country smithy, the corncake on a dewy morning, the sound of the scythe against the whetstone and the sight of a plough team coming over the brow of a hill. . . . The wild anemones in the woods in April, the last load at night of hay being drawn down a lane as the twilight comes on, when you can scarcely distinguish the figures of the horses as they take it home to the farm, and above all, most subtle, most penetrating and most moving, the smell of wood smoke coming up in an autumn evening or the smell of the scutch fires. . . . These are the things that make England.'[1] It was a more laconic but no less discerning worshipper who defined Scotland as 'porridge and heather and the Psalms of David'. And we may complete our trilogy with a more explicit document. 'Ireland? What is Ireland? Land? No. People? No. I am not ready to die for earth or for a people, a people which is not very different from other people. Ireland is something else. Ireland is the dead and the things the dead would have done; Ireland is the living and the things the living would die for. Ireland is the spirit. It is the tradition of undefeat, of indomitable failure.'[2] Not so explicit after all, perhaps, but anyhow its note is not that of a machine, nor its texture the texture of tape.

No doubt the cynic has a direct negative. All this is words and windy idealism. England is a mere abstraction, a 'geographical expression', an *ens rationis*. We can only reiterate that a society is a fact as 'hard' as any brickbat, vague as we have seen and indefinable—as are freedom and friendship and religion and truth. But these things are not words and breath; they are forces as real as electricity and considerably more dangerous. It was of such an armoury that Bradley was thinking when he said, 'Ink and paper can cut the throats of men and the sound of a breath may shake the world.' What does 'the State' mean? What *can* it mean? It is no objection that it does not exercise its power to the full on all its citizens, and on some it may exercise none. A magnet is none the less a magnet because it cannot attract mud. And a State which has no Haldanes or Brights, which can inspire fear and not

1. S. Baldwin, *On England*, pp. 6, 7.
2. F. Gallacher, *Days of Fear*, p. 93.

loyalty, is a carcass or an embryo. This, then, is the culmination of the power of the State, and any political theory that neglects it and finds the essence of political obligation in the Statute Book or the prison cell is moving, like the unhappy Achilles, 'a ghost among ghosts'.

(B)
The limits of State action

6

THE THEORIES LIMITING STATE ACTION

In the previous chapter we found how the theory of Rousseau easily developed into political absolutism, when we followed out the arguments which have led idealists to make the State the real liberator of man's moral nature, the single and dominant goal of his life, the supreme and unique focus of his loyalty and affection, and the source of all those institutions which differentiate him from the animals, and at the same time satisfy even his animal needs as no animal can ever satisfy them. If we were content to remain within the four corners of this vigorous creed, political authority would require no further defence. Any law which furthered the good of the State would be evidently right; we should legislate up to the hilt to prevent abuses and forward reform; a citizen could never evade the claim of the State to his obedience, nor could he ever rightly pursue any object other than the good of his community. We stated this position continuously and without qualification or misgiving, and we must now examine it point by point and attempt to retain only those elements in it which withstand criticism. This criticism falls under three heads:

(i) *Natural Rights and the Liberty of the Individual*

These theories attempt to find sacrosanct departments of human life where any interference is illegitimate.

(ii) *The immorality of compulsion and its destruction of character*

These theories attempt to show that the law destroys morality by removing choice and weakens character by eliminating responsibility.

(iii) *Non-political values and loyalties*

These arguments insist that some acts are right and some objects are good intrinsically, without reference to society; and further that the State is not the only embodiment of the common good.

We shall consider each of these groups in turn in the chapters which follow.

7

NATURAL RIGHTS AND THE
LIBERTY OF THE INDIVIDUAL

The first and historically the most interesting and important attempt to resist political absolutism is that which asserts the existence of Natural Rights. This is the view that each man has certain inalienable rights, which other men (and therefore the State) must respect and cannot assail. The theory has a more vigorous form, exemplified in Locke, which gives the State the positive duty of preserving these rights, but this advance leads at once to difficulties, for preservation and infringement are clearly inseparable. If the State is to ensure the protection of my property, whether I like it or not, it must have the right to attack it (by taxation, to finance its activities) whether I agree or not. If I am to have my right to free speech politically protected, the speech of those who would shout me down must have its freedom checked by the State. Were it not so obviously inadequate for anyone except Robinson Crusoe, the pure form of the theory is clearly more tenable than this development of it. The dilemma is most clearly seen in connection with the 'right to work' or the 'right to property'. These may be merely rights to retain whatever property I may have come to possess and to do whatever work I may find ready to hand, or they may be rights to claim from the State an adequate portion of property and a congenial type of work, rights which can be exercised only through vigorous State-interference in the general property or employment situation.

Fortunately, however, the niceties of the theory need not detain us if we attack it at its roots, and there it is most clearly vulner-

able. Natural Rights must be self-evident and they must be absolute if they are to be rights at all. For if a right is derivative from
a more fundamental right, then it is not 'natural' in the sense
intended; and if a right is to be explained or defended by reference
to the good of the community or of the individual concerned,
then these 'goods' are the ultimate values in the case, and their
pursuit may obviously infringe or destroy the 'rights' in question.
Now the only way in which to demonstrate the absurdity of a
theory which claims self-evidence for every article of its creed is
to make a list of the articles. The vague and haphazard and overlapping character of the famous lists of 1776 and 1789 needs no
further exposure. A glance at any newspaper correspondence will
show how elusive and how elastic the theory may become.[1]

Not only are the lists indeterminate and capricious in extent.
They are also confused in content. Is a 'right to life' distinct
from a right to liberty, to security or to happiness? Again there
is no single 'natural right', which is in fact regarded even by its
own supporters as sacrosanct. Every one of them is constantly
invaded in the public interest with universal approval. My life is
attacked by conscription, my liberty by health regulations, my
property by taxes for the education of the children of others,
my freedom of speech by the laws against indecency and slander.
Moreover, many of these rights defend institutions whose very
existence presupposes social organisation. It is only in social
setting that mere possession becomes 'property', that barter
becomes 'a wage', that non-interference becomes 'liberty', that
uninterrupted noise becomes 'free speech'. If these are all products
of social life they may surely be controlled in the general interest.

It may be said that a theory once so powerful cannot be wholly
absurd. The answer is that in the days of their greatness the 'rights
of man' were pleaded against privilege and oppression. They were
the weapons of the negro slave, of the Russian serf, or of the
English labourer. When a slave pleads the rights of man, he demands not freedom from the State but citizenship in it on the
same terms as his master. We must recall here two warnings we
have stressed before. In calling the theory we are criticising
'Absolutism' we made easy two misunderstandings: we risked a
confusion of it first with monarchy, second with oppression. Now

1. Six months' scrutiny of a correspondence column revealed a natural
right to a living wage, a right to work, a right to trial by jury, a right to buy
cigarettes after 8 p.m., a right to camp on a caravan by the roadside, and a
right to walk on the grouse moors of Scotland during the close season.

we pointed out in connection with Hobbes[1] that Absolutism has nothing to do with monarchy; it is a theory about the proper powers of government, however the constitution is organised. Moreover, Absolutism does not mean government in the interests of a certain class to the exclusion of others. Now it happens that in history Absolutism has usually been allied with one or both of these institutions—government *by* an exclusive group *in the interests of* an exclusive group; and this is the historical reason why 'natural rights' have had the distinguished career we noted. What we are now concerned to discover is whether they can resist an absolutism divorced from monarchy and oppression. What we find in fact is that as soon as monarchy and privilege disappeared from the institutions of the country, natural rights changed sides. Thus we had the curious development by which the sword of the revolutionary became the shield of the reactionary and the alarmed prophecy of Herbert Spencer was fulfilled.[2] We shall recur to this reversal below.[3]

We have seen the failure of lists of rights to secure a satisfactory basis for the theory; we must now turn to an attempt to set limits to State activity which sacrifices the sacrosanct independence of Natural Rights by reducing them all to one. This theory turns on the distinction between other-regarding and self-regarding actions. Its principle is that when my action affects only myself the State has no right to interfere with it. 'I am doing no harm to anyone else' is a complete defence. Clearly some of our correspondence-column rights[4] would be defended on these lines and are therefore not 'natural rights' independent of each other. The right to walk on grouse moors in July is not a different right from the right to walk on deer forests in April. Both are applications of the principle of 'doing no harm'. (Both are also, of course, invasions of the right of private property, but this is just the usual result we noted above, that the full claim of any one 'right' will always be found to be the invasion of all the others.) What are we to say, then, of the one right which remains to us, the right not to be interfered with in one's self-regarding actions? This is the theory of John Stuart Mill,[5] but we must not dismiss it as absurd for that reason only. Indeed, to many people, perhaps

1. Cf. p. 20.
2. 'If the present drift of things continues it may really happen that the Tories will be defenders of liberties which the Liberals in pursuit of what they think popular welfare trample under foot.' (*Man versus the State*, p. 17.)
3. See p. 62.   4. Cf. p. 58, *Note*.
5. *On Liberty*, ch. I (Everyman Edition, p. 73).

even to most people, it has exactly that forcible self-evidence
which is so conspicuously lacking in the other Natural Rights.

Now once again we must insist that if this is a genuine right it
must be self-evident and underivative. Mill confuses the issue by
quoting various good results which will accrue to a community
which leaves self-regarding actions alone. But this is a great logical
wickedness. It is like saying, 'It is self-evident that a thing is
either A or not A, and among the other evidence for it is the testi-
mony of Mansel and Jevons.' Many of Mill's 'secondary' arguments are sound and interesting and provide special reasons for
leaving free religious observance or scientific research. But they
can be addressed only to readers who reject entirely his main
theory, and require evidence for what is self-evident already. It
is to his main theory that we are now to attend. Of course, if the
theory is self-evident, we cannot quote evidence against it, nor
can we sit down comfortably and say it does not seem evident to
us. There are two ways of defeating it. One is to reject the distinction on which it turns. We may say that such apparently self-
regarding actions as drunkenness or drug-taking are really social
in effect. My family will suffer if I lose my health; or, if I have no
family, my servants will suffer by my example and my country
by my inefficiency. We might then cede the inviolability of self-
regarding actions with the comforting proviso that there are none.

This line of argument is a counsel of weakness, and corres-
ponds to the secondary arguments we condemned above. We may
pass it by with the comment that if anyone *still* thinks Mill's
principle self-evident (after our real argument, which follows) he
may try to get over this extra difficulty in his path.

But the other route to take against a self-evident maxim is to
find examples in which it does not seem to work. For myself I
should be satisfied with the 'drugs' example. I simply cannot feel
that my liberty is being unwarrantably assaulted by the laws
which stop the promiscuous sale of heroin even if my consumption
of it were to affect myself alone. Mill himself asks whether it is
justifiable to barricade a dangerous bridge. On his own arguments,
the most we can do is to placard and picket the bridgehead with
advice and exhortation. We ought not to use force. If there is no
time for warning Mill would use force, and he justifies it by
saying, 'Liberty consists in doing what one desires, and he does
not desire to fall into the river.'[1] Yet few would follow Mill in
limiting the use of barricades to this single extreme case.

1. *On Liberty*, ch. V (Everyman Edition, p. 152).

Herbert Spencer has this same view of liberty. 'The liberty the citizen enjoys is to be measured not by the governmental machinery he lives under, whether representative or other, but by the paucity of the restraints it imposes on him.'[1] Spencer saw what Absolutism or 'Totalitarianism' means, and that, if legislation as such is evil, its provenance (monarch or assembly) makes no difference. It cannot be ameliorated by a change to a democratic régime. He saw also that it is irrelevant whether the legislation is in the public interest or not. The evil of legislation cannot be cured by improving its effects. 'The motives were doubtless in nearly all cases good—we have here to concern ourselves solely with the compulsory nature of the measures.'[2] The opposite of Totalitarianism is neither democracy nor beneficent law, but *laissez-faire*.

Now I do not wish to deny that restraint as such is an evil. Restraint which has no good results at all is clearly bad, and if good results can be produced as well by methods of freedom as by methods of persuasion or force, then freedom is better than persuasion and persuasion better than force. What I am combating is the idea that restraint is an evil so great that, in whole fields of action (Natural Rights or self-regarding actions), no amount of good produced can counterbalance it. That it should be a factor to be taken into account in estimating action cannot be denied. And I can imagine cases where the good produced is so slight and the interference to produce it so widespread that legislation would be wrong.

Even here, however, I am still doubtful how far liberty is to be valued for itself and how far I am really counting on the ethical results discussed below and the good effects of variety and experiment to which Mill so often appeals. For if liberty itself is what I value it must have this high merit equally in the bad action and the good, and I cannot feel sure that, in a case where I knew I was doing wrong, it was at least one good element in the situation that no one tried to stop me and an element whose value is so high that for it alone innumerable people may be allowed to suffer and innumerable reforms be resisted.[3]

Note. While this is not a historical treatise it seems only fair, if the splendid history of the Rights of Man and the struggle for Liberty is to engage our attention, that, for counterpoise in the past and warning for the present, we should look for a moment

1. *Man versus the State*, p. 15.   2. Op. cit., p. 7.
3. See below, next para., for examples.

at the other side. We noticed how Absolutism has been confused
with monarchy and with oppressive privilege, and how especially
in England the cry of Natural Rights really rallied the opposition
against these latter foes. By 1832, however, in principle if not in
practice, these two enemies were finally destroyed. It was now
becoming recognised that the basis of our constitution was to be
universal democracy (with a few lingering anomalies), and it was
recognised that all classes of citizens must be considered and
benefited by legislation. It is the haunting echoes of those ancient
battles which still make our citizens think of government as an
external hostile force. But a cursory glance at the political literature of the last century will show the change to which I referred
above. It is no exaggeration to say that the Rights of Man and
the Liberty of the Individual—along with the plea we shall next
examine, the immorality of compulsion—have stood solidly
against every measure of reform and every attempt to promote
the public welfare. These doctrines were the principal foes of
education, vaccination, public health, slum removal, access to
mountains, free libraries, fair taxation, factory reform. The raising
of £10,000,000 for education was characterised by Herbert
Spencer as 'tyrannical'.[1] Mr O'Brien writes that Free Libraries
are 'founded upon theft and upon the violation of the most
sacred thing in the world, the liberty of your fellow man'.[2] The
attempt to mitigate conditions of labour in the nail-making
industry by appointing inspectors to report on them was attacked
as 'violating the sanctity of the English home'.[3] Even when
reports of the early commissions on mills and mines had rendered
some control inevitable the 'liberty of the individual' was hon-
oured by restricting the application of the reforms to the working
conditions of women and children, who were not really 'individuals' at all, and whose liberty to let themselves be poisoned or
paralysed (with starvation as the alternative) did not need to be
so meticulously preserved. In 1819 a bill was promoted to prohibit the use of small boys as chimney brushes. Speaking on this
bill, Lord Lauderdale said: 'Such things as this ought to be left
entirely to the moral feelings of perhaps the most moral people on
the face of the earth. . . . If the legislature attempts to lay down a
moral code for the people, there is always the danger that every
feeling of benevolence will be extirpated.'[4] The bill was accord-
ingly rejected.

1. *A Plea for Liberty*, p. 16.   2. Ib., p. 346.
3. Ib., p. 127.   4. Quoted Hammond, *Town Labourer*, p. 191.

8

THE IMMORALITY OF COMPULSION

A further objection to legislation is often found to lie in its incompatibility with moral behaviour. Every law deprives the citizen of a free choice and he is thereby debarred from acting morally or building up a strong character. Where there is no opportunity for vice there is no merit for virtue; 'better England free than England sober'. Law is not merely negative, removing opportunities for virtue; it is often positively evil, substituting a bad motive for a good one, and since the moral value of an action lies entirely in the motive the theory of Rousseau that, through law, the State 'sides with' my moral self is everywhere and entirely false. Every law marks the death of so much moral value. The State may make me abstain from some actions and do others, but between an act done from fear of prison and 'the same act' done from the right motive there is the whole difference between cowardice and courage, self-interest and self-sacrifice. The act is 'the same act' only in the sense that I 'go through the motions' as before. A body of persons living under a perfect legislative code might be clean, they might be efficient, they might conceivably be happy, but by no stretch of Platonic paradox could they, in virtue of their obedience to their code, be virtuous. It is to be particularly noted that this argument, while it holds against all legislation, is at its strongest against legislation which has as its object the removal of what is universally agreed to be evil. For only if the object to be removed is evil can the citizen be called on to resist it by his own efforts. A man will not strengthen his character by abstention from what is good or resistance to what is harmless. It is important to make this point strongly, for it is often confused with two others in any particular discussion. When a reputed evil is to be prohibited there will be some to say it is not an evil at all. (Gambling usually raises all these points.) But these same persons cannot use our present argument that it should be left free, to serve as a temptation to be resisted and an evil to be overcome. Others, again, will say the State is not in a position to decide what is evil and what is not, for this is not an 'expert' question, and people must answer it for themselves. But here again is a position incompatible with our present argument. It is only when an institution or activity is admitted by all parties to be evil that we can say, '*Because* it is evil, leave it alone, for removing evil makes virtue impossible.'

This same argument against removing evils by legislation is also used, *mutatis mutandis*, against supplying good things by State action, though with less vigour and violence, since the supply of good things does not usually strike vested interests so quickly and so clearly. When you provide by compulsion something of value, you cheapen it in men's eyes. It is a law of human nature— human nature is an open book, and an uninspiring one, to these theorists—that a man will not appreciate what he does not have to buy. Your legislation then destroys the merit of effort, it weakens independence and kills self-respect. Here, then, as before, the State is doomed. Every piece of good work it does destroys so much moral value. As before also, the better the work the greater the ruin. When the State took over the work of roadmaking it did not do much harm, for the reasonable pursuit of good roads is not a central virtue in human nature. But when it made education compulsory and free it destroyed at a blow all that sturdy independence and magnificent effort which, resting on a real desire for and appreciation of learning, counted nothing too much to pay for the privilege of the children's schooling. Now ('human nature' again 'being what it is') education is at best a mere routine and often a disagreeable necessity with the Attendance Officer and the County Court as its soulless instruments.

Now the *argumentum ad hominem* is inelegant criticism, but against a theory which can work only by imputing the lowest motives and making the worst of human nature it is perhaps less unjustifiable than elsewhere; and the natural reaction to such arguments is to say to their holders: 'Your own actions betray you. You do not consider it your duty to go about spreading disease and pain and squalor to give men an abundance of moral

[handwritten margin note:] This seems to be veiled has happened in the value of a degree now that 'grants' are available.

exercise (though your theory justifies a comfortable inertia about removing such things). You do not throw your own children on the gutter and leave your fortunes to your deadliest enemies that your children may become Spartan and your enemies soften and decay.' What justifies this tone and temper, at least in some cases, is that the use of these arguments seems to imply a capacity for vicarious moral endeavour in striking contrast with the actual inertia the theory is devised to defend.

The position, however, must be met by arguments more legitimate if we are to retain any belief whatever in the theories of Bosanquet and Rousseau. T. H. Green, after following out the idealist development to its logical conclusion, was compelled by exactly these arguments to retrace his steps and diminish the State's activities to a minimum. He was so convinced that every law is demoralising in its effect that his final formula is that the State can compel 'only those actions which are better done from a bad motive than not done at all'.[1] It is this certainty that all law is obeyed from bad motives that we must now set out to qualify.

We may begin with what is indubitably the strongest, though it may also be the rarest, case. Law may not act through fear alone. If we remember that it is possible for men to be reasonable but negligent, and if we reiterate that the cases we are considering are those of removing indubitable evils or promoting indisputable goods, it is obvious that a law may point out to a man an obligation he would have forgotten but will admit and welcome when it is brought to his notice. If the Medical Officer of Health discovers that his drains are disseminating disease, he may welcome the discovery and hasten to remove the offence. The motive here is not fear of prison but intelligent acquiescence. No doubt it is Utopian to suppose it at all widely effective. We are still, especially in this country, so steeped in the tradition and the memory of ancient and well-justified rebellion that our first instinct is to regard the Ministry of Health as John Hampden regarded Charles I—as an external and hostile tyrant whose behests are to be evaded or shelved or openly disobeyed. Yet there remains the potential rationality of man; and, however powerful our national prejudices may be, we should hesitate to erect a political theory on these alone. For it would be widely admitted that (although effective social legislation in England is hardly more than sixty years old) the attitude towards government is already changing

1. Green, *Principles of Political Obligation*, para. 15. And cf. even Bosanquet's similar suggestion (*Philosophical Theory of the State*, p. 191).

C

perceptibly, and law is beginning to acquire something of the regard which inherent merit should justify. This objection to *laissez faire* might be stated as a maxim for legislators thus: When you can see that your law is not only in the public interest but also so evidently and obviously in the public interest that those affected when they 'think twice' will see its value and necessity, then you can neglect entirely the argument about the immorality of compulsion and be sure that the law substitutes not a bad motive for a good one but a good one for a bad—viz. the enlightened pursuit of the public interest for blindness or ignorance or apathy. For present examples of such legislation we may think of much of our road traffic law or of the regulations under which dangerous trades are carried on—the loading of merchant ships or the transmission of electric power. Our objector may say these are unfair and negligible examples of law. But they are not—firstly because his arguments about the wrongness of compulsion were arguments against all law as such and any exceptions are equally fatal, and secondly because they are far from negligible, since in an economically developed society probably the bulk of legislation both in quantity and in importance must inevitably be found in such adjustments of interests and danger.

Further, when we are asked to think of law as acting solely through force and fear we should remember that, even if the intelligent acquiescence referred to above is Utopian and unusual when a law is first enforced, it may well follow quickly on enforcement. Many of those who might rebel against a new law and obey it only from all these bad motives may come to admit its merits when they have seen it working. Many doctors who resisted and attacked the Health Insurance Act when it was first proposed and who worked its provisions in a spirit of hostile and grudging acquiescence, would now admit that they were quickly convinced that the results were wholly good, and that they now carry out those regulations with no more feeling of enslavement than they have towards their stethoscopes or their 'Quain' or any other tried and trusted tool of their trade. We may quote once more that unguarded admission of the philosopher who did more than any other man to convince Englishmen that individualism was not only pleasant but also highly moral: 'Whatever cannot but be acknowledged to be of advantage to the society and people in general upon just and lasting measures will always, when done, justify itself.'[1]

1. Locke, Cf. above, p. 25.

Again, if we continue to work down the scale, away from the ideal case of a law welcomed and intelligently obeyed, we find a stage still short of force and fear. When a law has been passed abolishing an evil, its later history may not be that which we have just noticed in the Health Insurance Acts; it may be one in which early resistance is succeeded not by intelligent approval but by unconscious acquiescence, as the law becomes part of the settled order of the nation's life and the desire or temptation to break it simply disappears by <u>atrophy</u>. The maxim for legislators covering these last two cases is: <u>When you can foresee that the compulsive element is likely to be swiftly succeeded (as the reform 'proves itself') by intelligent welcome or—with the change of fashion—by unconscious acquiescence, then you can disregard the objections of the 'immoralists'</u>. Of course laws differ greatly in this respect. It seems unlikely that assault or libel or murder or blackmail should become obsolete owing to the effect of law passing into unconscious 'use and wont'. The laws against these offences will retain the element of compulsion. But <u>it is unlikely that anyone in England refrains from bear-baiting or from torture in fear of the police</u>. Even the education of children is probably now accepted as the 'natural' thing, and is not due nearly so much as in 1880 to the Attendance Officer. (In many areas he has been abolished.) A custom dies and a new one takes its place. One of the strongest points in favour of much of the legislation protecting animals is just this—that an enormous amount of the cruelty involved is the result of unconscious acquiescence due to simple ignorance or lack of imagination and continuing mainly through convention and fashion. When bear-baiting was abolished other entertainments took its place. The controls of the training of performing animals, of the trapping of animals for fur, of the making of *foie gras*, if enforced by law would cause only slight changes in what is at its best mainly caprice, the fashions of amusement or clothing or food. Animals which could be trained only by fear or trapped only with prolonged suffering would disappear from the circus and the fur market and in a year or two be forgotten altogether.

Two objections may be raised to such examples as this. First it may be said that if you abolish bear-baiting, all that happens is that something equally cruel like stag-hunting takes its place. This assumes that cruelty is a necessary element in the amusements of man; and even if it were we might hesitate before simple acquiescence in its satisfaction. Secondly, it may be said that a change of fashions is not a change of heart and there is no real advance in the morality of people who wear one fur, when another is unobtainable, for reasons they have forgotten or never known. This is a variant of the argument that the whole value of an action lies in its motive. But surely there is some value in the consequences, and if we had two communities equally dominated by fashion and ignorant of fact, one which followed harmless fashions would be preferable to one whose fashions caused needless suffering.

We have reviewed above a variety of situations in which the effect of law is not to substitute the motive of fear for the better motives of temperance and self-control. We may now ask: 'Who are the people on whom this bad motive is supposed to be effective in cases in which it is certainly operating? Who are kept from arson and slander solely by fear of the law?' Obviously only those who would commit arson or slander were detection and punishment avoidable. In these cases, then, the bad motive is substituted for a worse and not a better motive.

Note. In these discussions it would be an especial advantage if people would think concretely about the law. When the citizen's bondage to law is compared with that of a monk to his 'rule' and the consequent 'asceticism' and 'starvation of natural impulse' in the two cases attacked as immoral, this is largely due to mere lack of imagination. It would be better to take as an example *any one* citizen in any walk of life, and ask of him how often in a week his action is restricted by the State. It is only a genius for vicarious slavery that enables a man to develop the individualist case. I am compelled to send my children to school (not that I have any, and I should anyhow); I am unable to buy novocain (not that I want to); I am compelled to make lead-glaze by the 'fritting process' (I do not make lead-glaze); I am restrained from forestalling and regrating (whatever they may be); in short, I suppose no session passes but Parliament adds a round dozen to these pseudo-interferences with a liberty I do not covet, and I remain in fact as free as ever. Hegel's 'State' is sometimes accused of being the idol of a theory run mad. But the 'individual' of our present examination is no less of a chimera. An 'individual' on whom every law is a restriction, an 'individual' who, in the absence of all these laws, would be tempted by all the evils they abolish, yet fall to none, and by his own efforts resist them and so strengthen his character and further the good of his community at all these myriad points, such an 'individual' is the idol of a mythology which makes the hundred-eyed Argus and the hundred-handed Briareus sober biological specimens in comparison.

'The individual' who is at any rate nearer fact is one who is the slave of trusts and competition and inefficiency and who moves with enhanced freedom at every restraint that is placed on the murderous motorist, the short-weight shopkeeper or the confirmed forestaller and regrater.

9

NON-POLITICAL VALUES IN
MORAL ACTION

Conscientious motive and effort. Our first comment is supplementary rather than critical. Let us suppose for the moment that the right action is that which most effectively promotes the common good. Yet it is clear that the possession of this rightness will not render an action morally perfect.

In the first place we must consider the motive; and here we return to Kant and his insistence on the absolute value of the good will, of the action which is done *because* it is right. Now this is certainly a non-social value, because the action might have all the same good social effects and be done from a love of display or the hope of reward.

Further, this value need not even be additional to the social value but can subsist without it. For it is achieved not only when a man does what is right because it is right but also when he does what he *thinks* right. If in such a case his act does not promote the common good, 'owing to special disfavour of fortune or the niggardly provision of a step-motherly nature', it still has a moral value which no external accident can destroy. There is therefore an absolute and a non-social value in a man's doing what he thinks right for the sake of its rightness, whether it is right or not.

Suppose a man does not even succeed in doing what he thinks right (again owing to external nature or unavoidable ignorance or impotence). There will still be an element of unassailable moral value in his action if he *tries* to do it. This value again is independent of social context and results, and of the rightness of the action,

and may be possessed by an effort which actually achieves nothing
at all or nothing but harm.

A further development of the last point is that the effort of will
has a strength of its own which determines its value. When there
is temptation or strong resistance the effort set against it is the
measure of the man's merit.

These values are indubitable and definitely non-social and a
man certainly does his duty when his act embodies them.[1] For
'ought' implies 'can', and all a man can do is to try his best to do
what he believes is right, because he believes it right.

Yet such an analysis is obviously incomplete, for it leaves the
term 'right' undefined. In any actual crisis the question 'What is
the right act?' is that which alone interests the moral agent.
'Ought Regulus to have stayed in Rome?' This is ambiguous.
Strictly we must answer that it depends on what Regulus believed
to be the right action. If he believed it was right to return to
Carthage, then he did his duty when he turned back. But we may
still ask another question. Admitting that Regulus believed it was
right for him to return to Carthage, was his belief a true belief?
Was it really right? And this is the question Regulus himself must
first have asked. Holding the belief he did, he must certainly be
praised for his return. But the allotment of praise or blame is a
matter for the moral critic or the moral agent who looks back on
his action. In the actual situation his mind is set on a decision
between rival courses of action, any one of which may be thought
to be right, and not on the avoidance of blame. In other words,
every moral agent who says 'I ought to do what I think right'
reveals the fact that 'ought' and 'duty' are subjective terms but
that 'right' is objective.

Non-social goods. The most plausible simple definition of
'right' is 'productive of the common good'. Yet many men devote
much effort and perhaps even their whole lives to the attainments
of aims which are not social at all. The artist and the scientist
are not servants of the community but servants of beauty and
truth. If this sounds paradoxical, we must remember the essential
conditions for the achievement of social consequences are publication or practical application. If the work of the artist or the
scientist is justified only by his service to others, then his goal is
achieved not in the moment of creation or discovery but only in
the moment of communication or practical application. Whether

1. Cf. H. A. Prichard, *Duty and Ignorance of Fact* (Herz Lecture for the
British Academy, 1932).

this is true or not should be decided primarily on the evidence of the artists and the scientists themselves. Nor is there any doubt about the answer. It would be easy to find examples of purity of motive among these artists and scientists who have never wavered in their devotion to beauty or truth and have consistently regarded social consequences as irrelevant. But perhaps it will be most strikingly illustrated by the least likely cases among recent artists and scientists. No modern man of letters was more social and sociable or revelled more in his success than Arnold Bennett; yet he writes in his *Journals*:[1] 'I cannot conceive that any author should write as the de Goncourts say they wrote, "for posterity". An artist works only to satisfy himself and for the applause and appreciation neither of his fellows alive nor his fellows yet unborn. I would not care a bilberry for posterity. I should be my own justest judge from whom there would be no appeal; and having satisfied him (whether he were right or wrong) I should be content—as an artist. As a *man* I should be disgusted if I could not earn plenty of money and the praise of the discriminating.'

No recent scientist has done more for mankind than Louis Pasteur. Yet even in his work it is the fire of truth which in the end impresses us, and we may recall that no scene in his life reveals greater joy in achievement than his early discovery of the dissymmetry of tartaric crystals, the one discovery of his life which had no practical end to serve. No doubt the traditional Cambridge toast, 'Here's to Pure Mathematics! May she never be of any use to anybody', goes too far, but it enshrines sufficiently clearly the truth that the primary aim of the thinker is not to do good to his fellow-men.

A third candidate for recognition in this category is religion, if only it is admitted that religious experience is an end in itself and an experience which is essentially individual. Many no doubt would agree with Dr Marett[2] that, 'primarily and directly the subject, the owner as it were, of religious experience is the religious society, not the religious individual'. The questions whether worship is essentially corporate and whether a church is an end or a means are of course basic issues in theology and issues on which the sectaries divide; and all that can be said here is that any decision that religion is essentially corporate will shut out many mystics and contemplatives and will involve us in the paradox that no founder of a religion was himself religious until he had won a following.

1. 28 January 1897 (*Journals*, vol. I, p. 30).
2. Quoted by Bosanquet, *Philosophical Theory of the State*, p. 181, *Note*.

It is necessary, if we conclude that these activities are not social, to avoid the danger of calling them selfish. Truth and beauty transcend alike society and individual; they may call for sacrifice of self as indubitable as those of the soldier or the statesman, and a service as pure and disinterested. Here then the identification of morality with the service of society breaks down. Unless we are prepared to condemn as immoral, or at best misguided and self-deluding, lives which are devoted to truth or beauty or worship, we must admit that here are ideals which our social standard fails to measure.[1] If we are to retain any belief in the theory of the idealists that morality is the immanent working in man of a spirit in which human personality finds self-fulfilment it must be belief in a spirit which transcends States and their frontiers and which speaks to the mind of man no less through the moods of nature and her laws than through Church or Law. This conclusion is fortified by a point which must be considered more fully below. The service of society itself presupposes that there are things which are intrinsically good without reference to society. For my aim of doing to others will lack determinate direction and content unless I consider health or knowledge or beauty to be good. My recognition of their goodness is therefore prior to and independent of any consideration of the particular people among whom I propose to disseminate them. When I work to make a town healthy, the health I bring about is not made valuable by being enjoyed by these particular persons.

Among the non-social goods which we are considering is one which requires special care in a work on political theory, and that is freedom. In an earlier section some consideration was given to the attempts to use the goodness of freedom as an argument against State interference, and it was shown that in the special

1. The closing pages of T. H. Green's *Prolegomena to Ethics* show once more the conflict in him between his idealist theory of the common good and his honest recognition of non-social values. He is speaking of the justification of a life devoted to music, and he says that unless there are special claims on a man 'the main question will be of his particular talent. Has he talent to serve mankind—to contribute to the perfection of the human soul—more as a musician than in any other way?' The suggestion in this sentence that it is the souls of others which his work must perfect is at once belied by the sentence which follows, where the supreme value of music is said to be 'enabling him to share in that intrinsically valuable lifting up of the soul which music may afford'—where 'share in' is clearly only a misleading phrase for 'experience' or 'enjoy'. Bosanquet in the closing pages of his book (which contain admissions which conflict with much of his general theory) does full justice to these non-social values. (*Philosophical Theory of the State*, pp. 332–3.)

forms this argument took ('Natural Rights' and 'self-regarding actions') it broke down. A 'Natural Right' can be no more than a claim to perform a certain sort of action or enjoy a certain sort of institution because this action or this institution is necessary to achieve a good. And this claim will be threatened if alternative means to the same good can be found and its absoluteness can never be maintained against the competition of greater goods. It was found impossible to trace any *self-evidence* in the claim for self-regarding actions and it was pointed out that the use of *other* evidence in fact relinquished the claim. But the admission was then made that there was an element of value in freedom itself wherever it is found. Freedom here means action not motivated by fear of others and particularly the ability to choose action A without the pressure of threats by others aimed at preventing me from doing A or getting me to do B through fear of the consequences, which they will bring about if I do A or omit B. This is a narrow definition of freedom. For I do not think my freedom is in the same sense interfered with by fear of 'physical consequences' nor generally by fear of causal consequences. If I say to myself, 'Suppose I do A, I shall be unpopular', this is no limitation on my freedom. The consequences which I wish to avoid if I am to have the freedom I am now claiming are (i) consequences predicted by others as likely to follow my action; (ii) consequences whose prediction is meant to dissuade me from so acting; (iii) consequences whose occurrences will be due to those who make the predictions with the intentions indicated in (ii). I think anyone would recognise the distinction between this 'interference' and the previous 'limitations'. Limitations put upon me by the structure of the world, by my own powers, by the nature of others, these form the necessary setting for any decision. But limitations directly thrust upon me through the intentional choice of others are 'interferences', and the direct assault of the personality of others upon my own.

That such freedom is intrinsically good is implied by the admission I made above that, other things being equal, persuasion is better than threats.[1] But we must recall the warnings given above. Firstly, if freedom is intrinsically good it is not to be defended by its effects. To say freedom makes possible experiment and discovery would justify the constraint of those whose use of their freedom involves no discoveries. Secondly, if freedom is intrinsically good it is not to be limited to special fields, such as

1. J. P. Plamenatz, *Consent, Freedom and Political Obligation, ad. fin.*

those of Natural Rights, self-regarding actions, conscience, truth or religion. *Whatever I do*, the characteristic of my action that it is not done under threats is an element of good in it, an element to be found equally in the actions of the drunkard, the embezzler, the golfer, the hero and the saint. Similarly, whatever I do under threats, no matter how good I am or how beneficial my action, has an element of evil in it.

These conclusions must be accepted, but their consequences should show that the goodness of this freedom is very slight indeed, that when it stands alone it can weigh little in the scales of our decisions. When it can be supplemented in special cases, as in Religion or Truth, by a value derived from the merits of these cases, then of course freedom weighs very heavily in our decisions.

Here, however, no detailed decisions are possible. What the reader should do is to discover whether he himself admits the principle that freedom as defined above can be distinguished from the other senses, and that when so distinguished it can be recognised as intrinsically good. Even if this is admitted, it seems to be a good which is not great enough to be made the centre of a political theory, nor so great that much else of intrinsic value must be sacrificed for it.

There are some non-social goods, such as health, which may nevertheless be promoted by State action. But those we have here been considering in detail cannot be so controlled. There is an old story of a bishop who congratulated an Oxford head on the attendance at college chapel. The head said, 'Yes, chapel is compulsory.' The bishop raised his eyebrows. The head continued: 'Things have come to such a pass that it has become a choice between compulsory religion and no religion at all.' The bishop replied: 'My mind is not subtle enough to see that distinction.' Compulsory religion is a contradiction in terms. Totalitarian States have tried to direct religion according to their political ends, or even to supply a religion (e.g. the 'old Germanic religion') specially adapted for this purpose. Such attempts are self-defeating. The only logical attitude for a State which fears the rival loyalty which religion can claim is that of the early Bolsheviks and the orthodox Marxists: religion as such is evil and to be destroyed. If the State attempts to control doctrine or dictate forms of worship it must be for some reason other than the proper ends of doctrine and worship—namely truth and holiness. But to be ordered to believe a doctrine for a reason other than its truth or to worship for any end other than holiness is a self-contradiction—like an order to swim without water, or to breathe without oxygen. This position is not concerned with the question of authority within a Church. It may be a part of my religious belief that I must bow to authority but it must be a religious authority. If my doctrine requires it or my mind is confused, I may take advice or aid or even instructions from superiors, but they must be spiritual superiors—men who are making truth and holiness their ultimate good, as I am.

A similar argument applies to learning. In this field too State-dictated or State-controlled belief is a self-contradiction. Learning and research, science and philosophy are free or they are nothing. The degradation of the German mind must have gone far if Germans could read without a smile that Herr X was returning to South-West Africa 'after having received instruction in the new German racio-biology'. As with religion, so with learning. The Nazi Government tried to harness it to the State. But the clearer-sighted Nazis recognised the impossibility and took the more logical view that reason is evil. 'The heart' or 'the blood' should guide action; the example of the leaders bore this out. 'I go my way like a somnambulist' (Hitler); 'I am like the beasts. I smell the weather before it changes. If I trust to my instincts I never err' (Mussolini). The Nazis also believed that, if they could not control learning, they could at least control teaching. But what sort of teaching is it that is divorced from learning? So far as the content of German teaching was controlled, the teacher had necessarily to be a knave or a tool.

The third value which will not brook control is beauty. Here again the logical attitude is that of the puritan who holds that beauty as such is evil. The attempt to harness and use art under external direction is a self-destructive and self-defeating one. It was no accident that the exhibition of 'pre-Nazi Germany' in New York included all that was best in German art, literature, music and drama, and was entirely the work of men who became martyrs or exiles under the Nazi régime. The case of beauty is, however, not quite so simple as the other two. For any régime which rests at all on emotional enthusiasm and harnesses to any degree a spirit of service, however misguided, will throw up occasionally an artist who honestly feels and can therefore effectively express the emotion and enthusiasm. The early Russian films show how even a narrow and childish enthusiasm—a worship of tractors and fat stock—can express itself in beauty. And the more recent Russian films show how much of this early faith and idealism has been lost. Moreover, the best of these early films belonged to the NEP period of relaxed stringency; it therefore seems that some freedom of the spirit was needed even for the work of Pudovkin and Eisenstein. And even this narrow success is won at the cost of sacrificing all else—all enthusiasms other than the official line, all art not directly useful as propaganda.

The State can supply external conditions in which learning and religion and beauty may develop—universities, schools, art galleries, concert halls. But it cannot directly produce or control these values themselves. Here then are claims to freedom which may stand unchallenged.

Common good with no community. Even when we have surrendered the claims of 'social service' in the fields of non-social value discussed above, further surrender is still necessary. The duties of fidelity to promises, of payment of debts, of the saving of life are not the service of any society or community. For they are owed to other men regardless of their race or tribe. 'Keeping of faith belongs to men as men and not as members of society.'[1] I believe I ought to pay my German bookseller or to tell the truth to a Frenchman who asks me the way from Fiume to Susak. Any theory which, like Hegel's, shuts morality within a frontier will be unable to explain these duties. Yet Hegel is often corrected by critics who invoke a mythology wilder than Hegel's own. They say that the Idealists attribute to the State claims and characteristics which really belong to 'Society'. When my duties of truth and fidelity are attributed to my relations to 'Society', this must result in one of three views. 'Society' may be the name of the totality of human beings with whom I am actually related either consciously[2] or unconsciously[3] in ways which affect my own life. But there are men with whom I am not yet in any relationship, and to whom I should have duties under certain conditions. To include all those to whom I might have relations involving duties or rights we cannot stop short of the whole human race. The whole of humanity is then that greater 'Society' to which I really owe allegiance and whose common good I serve.[4] But it is clear that the whole human race is in no sense a Society, just as all red-haired men and all sufferers from rheumatism are not

1. Locke, *Second Treatise on Civil Government*, ch. II, para. 14 (Works, 1823, vol. IV, p. 346).
2. This seems to be the view of R. Maciver. See further below.
3. This is suggested by the treatment of G. Wallas. Cf. *The Great Society*, ch. I.
4. This is T. H. Green's view. See further below.

Societies,[1] and this leads to our third solution. The whole human race is not yet a Society, but it ought to be. Therefore when I perform my duties to a fellow-man we are both members of an ideal Society which lies ahead and whose common good would be realised were all its members determined by these rules of truth, fidelity, etc.[2] In order to see the difficulties of these views I shall examine in greater detail the treatment of them by some authorities on political theory.

Maciver begins his enquiry by deploring the inaccuracy of our sociological terminology. He then proposes to distinguish three terms—society, community and association—and to attach to each a special and accurate significance. 'Society,' he says, 'I intend to use in a universal or generic sense to include every willed relationship of man to man; community, state and association as special kinds or aspects of social fact.'[3] This ought literally to mean that 'Society' is a general term, the name given to any one of the various groups to which a man may belong, and that communities, States and associations are different species of Society, just as colour is a genus whose species are red, blue, etc. This usage would be free from misleading features (though, as I shall show below, the term 'association' would be adequate and even safer). But Maciver's further use of the term 'Society' issues partly in an awkward and unwarrantable extension of this meaning and partly in a confusion. For, as his definition shows, he must regard any persons who stand in a willed relationship as constituting *eo ipso* a society. My German bookseller and I form one society and my Frenchman in Fiume and I another. But this is obviously a misuse of language so extreme as to confuse rather than clarify social theory. What is still more fatal to accuracy is that Maciver writes (and on occasion thinks) as if 'Society' had quite a different meaning. He then uses 'Society' as a *singular* term, as if there were only one entity whose name is 'Society', but many States, associations, etc. There are traces of this even in his definition, where he says that Society 'includes' associations or that they are 'aspects' of it. Colour does not include blue nor is blue an aspect of colour. He has here

1. Bosanquet himself (*Philosophical Theory of the State*, pp. 328–32) accepts the existence of duties of man to man as underived from any Society or common good and is here clearer than most of those who criticise him.

2. This is Mr Joseph's view (*Some Problems in Ethics*, ch. IX, especially pp. 118, 119). Green also occasionally approaches it, though he thinks the ideal is already partially achieved (*Prolegomena to Ethics*, paras. 259, 280).

3. *Community*, p. 22.

slipped over from the relation between genus and species, which is harmless, to that between part and whole, which is fatal. In such statements as 'Society is nothing more than individuals associated and organised',[1] or 'Certain religious doctrines may undermine the security of society,'[2] or 'The interests of the individual are the interests of society',[3] the danger is obvious. We have here an instance of exactly that fallacy which Maciver himself attributes to Bosanquet, the fallacy of supposing that a collection of minds is a collective mind or a collection of trees a big tree. All the societies in the world do not together make up 'Society'.

Maciver would defend the use of 'Society' as a generic term on the ground that two of its species, communities and associations, are very different from each other and yet have something in common. I hope to show that 'Community' is really no more a genuine unit than is 'Society' when used in the dangerous singular sense condemned above. According to Maciver, the essential difference between a community and an association is that an association is organised and a community is not. A community is defined as 'an *area* of common life, village or town or district or country or even wider area'.[4] The common life 'must have some characteristics of its own such that the frontiers of the area have some meaning'.[5] The inhabitants of the area must resemble each other. Now here again there seem to be confusions and the same cardinal error. In the first place, the insistence on an 'area' and a 'frontier' is contradicted by such examples as that of the Jews or by Maciver's own example immediately following his definition, that of the English residents in a foreign capital, for he would have to hold that these residents do not constitute a community unless they live in an 'English Quarter'.[6] But if unity is not given to the community by its area, where else may we look? Similarity will not help us, otherwise all red-haired men would be one community and all rheumatics another. It is indeed clear that when we speak of the English community in Florence we mean more than the aggregate of Englishmen who live in Florence, for we should not call them a 'community' unless they were aware of each other's existence and took some pleasure in each other's company because of their common nationality. Even these minimal conditions seem to be lacking in another of Maciver's examples. He says that Western Europe is a community[7] and here the 'common life' can be no more than mere similarity. To say

1. Ib., p. 69.   2. Ib., p. 40.   3. Ib., p. 90.   4. Op. cit., p. 22.
5. Ib., p. 22.   6. Ib., p. 23.   7. Ib., p. 38.

that men form a community when these conditions are found is surely to restate the facts in a misleading way and not to name a unit resulting from them. For if we are to justify the use of 'community' as the name of a social unit, we must find some statements about communities which are not directly and obviously analysable into statements about their members, Maciver sees this and gives a list of epithets which belong to communities, namely 'nomadic, barbarous, civilised, populous, war-like, or again caste-ridden, feudalised, industrialised'.[1] But it is clear that 'caste-ridden' and 'feudalised' apply to the organisation of the society in question, which would therefore be an association and not a community; and the rest, with one exception, are characters of the inhabitants. The exception is 'populous' and it proves the rule; for, if it simply means numerous, the aggregate of red-heads could obviously be called more populous than that of rheumatics, and, if it indicates a high proportion of population to area, England north of the line from Trent to Severn could well be more populous than England south of that line without either England being constituted a community thereby. What, then, are the facts which we misleadingly state when we talk of the Jewish community or the English community in Florence? First, that Jews are similar in many respects; second, that Jews find pleasure in each other's company and tend to help and understand each other as Jews and non-Jews might not. But this may result from any similarity. Tailors or diabetics are similar to each other in various ways, and men naturally tend to take an interest in and to get on easily with those with whom they have much in common. But if we are to say that wherever such a group of facts is observed we have a specimen of a special type of social unit we shall be multiplying entities without necessity and finding ourselves compelled to include the diabetic community and the tailoring fraternity among them.

In his *Introduction to Social Theory* Professor Cole devotes two chapters to an analysis of terms. He agrees with Maciver in his use of 'community', but he says that 'every *community* may be regarded as giving rise to an organised *Society*'.[2] A Society is 'the complex of organised associations and institutions within the community'.[3] It is surely clear that the justification of treating a Society so defined as a unit is entirely dependent on the interpretation of the word 'complex'. Let us allow for the moment that England is a community. Then the Miners' Federation, mono-

1. Op. cit., Appendix (3rd ed.), p. 422.   2. Ib., p. 25.   3. Ib., p. 29.

gamy, the MCC, hire-purchase and the Poultry Fanciers' Association are items in the 'complex of associations and institutions' which is to be found in England. But in what sense do they together constitute a single unit? If Cole had said 'aggregate' instead of 'complex' the fallacy would be avoided, but the term 'Society' would be abolished. It is also to be observed with what dangerous ease he passes from the view that a Society is made up of organised units to the suggestion that it is itself an organised unit. 'Society is a complex of organised associations'[1] then gives place to 'Society is the sum total of organised social structure'[2] and that seems in turn to justify 'A *community* gives rise to an organised *Society*.'[3] No doubt the State is itself 'organised', but Cole would be the first to deny that the State includes churches, universities, etc.,[4] and there is no other organised unit which does include them. I would therefore maintain that there is no defence for the use of this term 'Society' as one of the types of unit with which sociology has to deal. I find neither in Cole nor in Maciver any necessity for the term at all. All its uses by philosophers and political theorists seem to me dangerously misleading. I think the adjective 'social' is harmless as describing relationships of all sorts between man and man. But its derivative 'Society' should be banished in the interests of clear thinking. Friendship and indebtedness are social relationships, but neither do friends nor do debtor and creditor compose societies.

Cole, as I said above, accepts Maciver's use of 'community'. But he is more sensible than Maciver of the considerations I urged above which would require the rejection of 'community' as a social unit also. He sees that if we look at a community objectively—from the outside as it were—it is hard to believe that it is a unit at all. All we can discover is a number of men similar in customs and traditions, and able and ready to help one another because they are of a common race or talk the same language or worship the same idols. Cole's remedy is not to give up 'community' as a social unit, but to say it is a 'subjective social unit'. It is 'a group felt by its members to be a real and operative unity'.[5] 'The reality of it *consists in* the consciousness of it among its members.'[6] Now this is a very interesting additional point. It is not enough that Englishmen should be conscious that other

1. Op. cit., p. 29. 2. Ib., p. 30. 3. Ib., p. 25.
4. See his article *Loyalties* (Proceedings of the Aristotelian Society, 1925–6).
5. *Introduction to Social Theory*, p. 28. 6. Ib., p. 26 (my italics).

Englishmen speak the same language, believe in monogamous marriage, dislike State-interference, etc. They must also believe in England—believe that there is a unity, believe that it is operative—and then, since in the end sociology is dealing with psychological facts, the belief will create the fact (as Tinker Bell is kept alive in *Peter Pan* by the beliefs of the children in the audience). Now any full answer to this would lead us very deep into the metaphysics of thought and its object. The most I can do is to indicate the difficulty by a parallel. The error of a sociologist who imports a 'subjective social unit' seems to me like the error a theologian would make if he included the Devil as a theological reality with the proviso that he was a 'subjective theological reality'. Individual persons have believed in a Devil, yet the theologian may maintain that their evidence was poetry misinterpreted as history and that the belief itself involves great difficulties. Therefore the Devil is no reality at all. So I agree that individual persons have believed that their own races or communities were realities, but I think I can show the logical and psychological errors in which this belief originated and also the further errors to which it in turn would give rise. If men 'feel their community as a real and operative unity' they are just wrong as an animistic savage is just wrong. Whenever they think it acts or suffers, the act or suffering is really that of individuals; whatever they believe about it is either a false belief about it or a disguised true belief about individuals. No doubt their belief that their race or community is a unit will make their actions different from what they would be without the belief, and it is just this difference which tempts the observer to believe that they constitute a unit of a new kind. But believers in a devil or in a banshee will also behave differently from non-believers, and yet their beliefs may be false.

I maintain therefore that there is only one type of social unit and that is the organised association. 'Association' will then serve as our generic term, with churches, States, clubs, etc., as its species. Then 'Society', with all its misleading implications, may be banished from our vocabulary. It is clear that our temptations to say 'We are all members of Society,' or 'We have duties to Society', or to use phrases like 'the security of Society', would all be removed if we substituted in these cases the term 'association' for 'Society.' The accusation levelled against Hegel, that he attributed to the State characteristics which really belong to Society, must now be more accurately restated, in the form that he attributed to man's relations to the State certain duties and rights which hold between men as men with no basis in any association, and also that he maintained that the State was the only or at least the highest association, attributing to it the fostering and maintenance of institutions which may be maintained more effectively by other associations.

T. H. Green shows here as elsewhere the struggles of a liberal individualist to avoid being driven into Hegelianism. He attempts to find a way out by conceiving of a loyalty wider than the political loyalty because it is felt to a society larger than the State. He regards moral progress as 'the extension of the range of persons for whom the common good is conceived as common'.[1] The Athenian did not do justice to the 'barbarian', nor did the Roman to his slave. Only with Christianity was the widening process complete. 'The idea has been formed of the possible inclusion of all men in a society of equals and much has been done towards its realisation.'[2] Yet he can speak in the same context of 'a duty of man to man as such and not merely as the member of a community',[3] and he shows how the tendency to speak of these human duties as if they were dependent on membership of some great society may have had its rise in a false analogy. 'The language in which we most naturally express our conception of the duty of all men to all men indicates the school—that of tribal, or civil, or family obligation—in which we have been trained to the conception. We convey it in the concrete by speaking of a human family, of a fraternity of all men, of the common fatherhood of God, or we suppose a universal Christian citizenship, as wide as the Humanity for which Christ died, and in thought we transfer to this under certain analogical adaptations those claims of one citizen upon another which have actually been enforced in societies united under a single sovereignty.'[4] When we consider the change which widened the conception of city loyalty to that of national loyalty in Greece, or the change which accompanied recognition of the rights of slaves, we see that it was, speaking quite accurately, a *political* change. The Greek cities lost their autonomy; slaves became citizens. If we now ask what is the ideal which Christianity requires as the social accompaniment of the recognition of the rights of man, we find once again that Green's language is guarded. He is not prepared to follow the movement of his own thought to its logical outcome. For that would lead him to the notion of a World-State actually enforcing

1. *Prolegomena to Ethics*, para. 206.   2. Ib., para. 280.   3. Loc. cit.
4. Op. cit., para. 206.

these wider duties through a single sovereignty—a State in which particular nations should have relinquished· their sovereignty. What he actually says, however, is this: 'For those citizens of Christendom on whom the idea of Christendom has taken hold, such a society does actually exist. For them—according to their conscientious conviction, if not according to their practice —mankind is a society of which the members owe reciprocal services to each other, simply as man to man. And the idea of this social unity has been so far realised that the modern State, unlike the ancient, secures equality before the law to all persons living within the territory over which its jurisdiction extends and in theory at least treats aliens as no less possessed of rights.'[1] We see here that he has in mind an alternative answer, and one in which a World-State is not necessary to provide a basis for the duties of man to man.

Goods social but not political. A further point has emerged in the course of the last discussion. Even in the cases where I am serving an association, that association need not be the State. There are other societies to which loyalty is felt and lives are dedicated. The problem of the relation between the State and these other associations will be discussed in a later chapter, and here only a few dogmatic conclusions may be anticipated. The most deep-seated and demonstrable error of the theorists of State supremacy and of their Fascist or Totalitarian successors is their inevitable attempt to reduce to political terms activities such as art, learning and religion, which are not even social, still less political, an attempt which destroys the values which it would control. But it is only less of an error when a government attempts to harness to political or national or racial purposes activities which are naturally social, such as trade or sport. For these activities are then pursued with a falsity of purpose and a perversion of spirit which destroy their significance. There are few more depressing chapters in the history of any fine human achievement than the irruption of national rivalry into mountaineering, a rivalry which enabled careless folly and suicidal haste, which would previously have been branded as criminal selfishness, to masquerade as national honour. 'A most undesirable feature of competition and rivalry had appeared in Alpine climbing since 1914 and had greatly increased during recent years. . . . Fickert and Hermann (two Teutonic guideless climbers) tracked us in 1930 up to the Jägerjoch, travelling unroped on crevassed and

1. Ib., para. 280.

snow-covered glacier. When we expostulated, they replied, "We Germans only use the rope on rocks," and looked at me scornfully. . . . They were last seen alive a day or two later when going up to try the E. face of the Rothorn, and probably fell into a crevasse."[1]

'Since 1930 a dismal series of fatalities upon its *verglas*-coated storm-swept slabs and overhangs [the North Face of the Grand Jorasses] has stained Alpine history. The sensational press has taken it up and articles under such headings as "*Un émouvant duel franco-allemand*" are turning the conquest of this terrible wall . . . into an international struggle. Hitler is alleged to join in with telegrams of condolence to the relatives of perished young climbers, celebrating each "*fait d'héroisme accompli en territoire étranger*". More lamentable even than the deaths or the waste of so much courage is this corruption of a sport which once promoted sympathy and understanding between peoples.'[2]

The common good analysed. So far we have accepted from ordinary speech the phrases 'common good' and 'social service' and have been concerned only to show that, even if they are thus accepted, there are moral claims and situations to which they are inapplicable. We must now attempt to analyse these notions themselves; for, even when they are normally applied, there is frequently little or no justification for their use. There seems to me to be at least seven different senses of 'common good'.

(i) When we say that anything is a good common to a number of persons we may mean simply that each has achieved for himself a good similar to that achieved, also for themselves, by all the others. Here the use of 'common' or 'general' is that which is found also in such phrases as 'our common humanity', 'the common cold', 'general distrust' or 'a general rise in temperature'. It is obvious that if twelve men working independently acquire each a piece of information, or a cold, or anything else, their achievement does not turn them into a community or a society, nor does the nature of each man's success depend in the least on the success of the others, nor is their good in any sense one good. In this usage, then, the phrase has no significance.

(ii) We may, however, speak of a man as setting before himself

---

1. T. Graham Brown, *Brenva*, p. 150. And compare pp. 205–6 for a further delicious description of the 'strange contradictions' of inter-war Teutonic mountaineering, including its 'widespread tendency to climb to the gallery'.
2. D. Pilley, *Climbing Days*, p. 193.

a 'common good' when he recognises something as good and
attempts to confer it on others, for instance when a man who has
found relief from suffering in a drug gives the drug to a fellow-
sufferer. Once again, however, as we saw above, this duty has
nothing to do with any community or society. 'Common good' is
still a misleading phrase. The good—relief from pain—is enjoyed
by individuals, and produced by individuals for individuals.

(iii) In certain cases men achieve their own private ends or
even the good of other men by means of an organisation which
is genuinely common to them all, in a sense in which the good
it achieves is not. When you employ the same secretary as I do,
the secretary is not multiplied thereby, but when you catch my
cold there are two colds and not one. But there is a further result
of this organisation. The good achieved becomes both extended
and limited. It is extended to all other members of the society
and also made continuous for them, but it is limited to these other
members also. If a rich man is impressed by the suffering of
certain children from lack of air and sunlight and presents a park
to a town, the good he will do is no longer limited to the particular
children whom he first saw but extends to all children in that
town. It is a good which will be achieved not only so long as he
is thinking of their welfare but which will go on continuously
while he sleeps and after he has forgotten. Yet it is also limited,
for he may see suffering children in the next town and have no
longer any funds left for their relief. It is clear that while the
phrase 'common good' is still literally inapplicable, there is at
last some justification for its use. Although the goods themselves
(health and relief from pain) are still private and many, the machinery (the park) is genuinely common and one, and the extent
and incidence of the goods are different from what they would be
without the machinery. So the element which is common makes a
difference to the elements which are good.

(iv) In this last case the common machinery—property or
organisation—achieved more adequately (both in continuity and
in extent) than private enterprise the good of the persons concerned. Yet it was not essential that the good should be achieved
in that way. The rich man might have brought successive parties
of children to his own park. In some cases, however, the machinery
must be common if the ends are to be achieved at all. The good
achieved by traffic control or credit regulation or civil law is of
this type. Physical safety, financial security, commercial stability,
these cannot be achieved at all by private enterprise without social

organisation. Yet, though here what is common is essential to what is good, the machinery (which is common) is not good and the safety and confidence (which are good) are not common.

(v) In all the cases above the good achieved was achieved for individuals, and the fact that one individual possessed the good made it intrinsically no more likely that any other would. In certain instances, however—that of infectious disease, for example —the achievement of health by individuals in an unhealthy community is impossible. It is not mere general assistance to a number of men taken separately which is the aim of a medical officer who attempts to establish a general standard of sanitation; it is the recognition that the good which sanitation achieves must be enjoyed by all members of a community if it is to be securely possessed by any. Clearly 'common good' is applied even more plausibly in such cases as this. Some hint of the same meaning lurks in the phrase 'common knowledge', which would normally suggest not merely that many men all know the same fact but that communication and not private enterprise led most of them to that knowledge. Yet here again the knowledge (like the good in the case of sanitation) is still essentially each man's separate knowledge. My escape from diphtheria is my good, even if in order to achieve it I have to see that others are free from diphtheria also.

(vi) In all the cases dealt with above there has been found no real justification for the association of 'common' with 'good'. Any factor which was really common was merely a means to the private good of individuals. The next case is one in which the common factor seems more than a means. When men recognise that co-operation with others is the best way to achieve an end, and when they form an association to achieve it, each member of the association feels more interests in the good of his associates than 'he would feel in mere fellow-men. The real problem is whether this psychological fact has any moral significance, whether I ever have a *duty* to promote the good of another person because he is a member of the same association as myself, a duty which I should not have to anyone who was not a member. Should charity begin at home?

It is difficult to give a conclusive answer to this question. Argument seems out of place and experience equivocal. There seem to be instances in which the claims of fellow-members of associations give rise to indubitable duties and others in which their claims have no weight or a weight which would disturb the balance of the moral decision. If a member of my own college asks me for advice or information about a career, I feel an obligation which would be weaker if he belonged to another college and non-existent if he were a man in the street. If a fellow of my college is writing about the theology or literature and asks for advice on a philosophical point, I feel I owe him a degree of help which I should not owe to a Cambridge scholar or an American theologian. Yet if I am asked to support a member of my own college or university in an academic or political election I feel the corporate claim may be a distraction. If, instead of attempting to consult my own feelings, I follow the Aristotelian precept and consult those of my friends for whose judgment I have most respect, I find just the same divergence. Men equally scrupulous and fair give contradictory decisions. Some say that the existence of an association such as a college gives fellow-members a claim on each other, and they would even override my scruples about the election example. Others say that charity may begin at home only when it is able so to be the more effective, but that any other recognition of fellow-members is immoral (except where there are special responsibilities of office). In the instance above concerning advice on careers, if I were the man's tutor, or if I were the college appointments officer, I should have a special duty, but this would derive from my office and not from membership of the college. On the whole I incline to the belief that membership does not constitute a claim and that there is some special feature about the instances in which the claim ought to be disregarded, an overriding negative duty of impartiality or something of that sort. In any case this is clearly a difficult problem and one of the first importance, especially at a time when conflicting loyalties provide the most prevalent moral problems, and when to some men loyalty seems the highest virtue and to others a mere savage superstition.

To return to our analysis, it need only be observed that, even if the above difficulty is resolved in favour of the claims of membership, the good is still not itself common or corporate; it is the good of individuals, though of these special individuals in virtue of their membership of my association. The salient difference from all previous cases is that it is my membership of the association which constitutes the good of the members a claim on me.

(vii) The other category in which 'common good' seems more defensible than elsewhere is that in which the good itself at last ceases to be private in its nature but is a state of affairs involving relations between individuals, a state of affairs intrinsically social. Here the social relations are not means or machinery for the production of good but themselves the good at which men aim. If five men co-operate to help a sixth it is probable that he will be helped more efficiently, but besides this advantage there will come into existence the condition of willing co-operation, which is itself intrinsically good. It is some recognition of this intrinsic value which we miss in attacks on the family, whether modern or Platonic. If you treat the family merely as a means to the production of a good stock (as did Plato), or to the education and nurture of the children (as do some moderns), then you will be tempted to find, in a combination of sterilisation and selective eugenics, or in a crèche system, some better machinery to serve your ends. But, unless you could replace in your new system the close-knit sympathy and understanding of which at its best the family is capable, you will lose something of intrinsic worth. Similarly a school or college is not a mere piece of machinery to enable A, B and C to teach and X, Y and Z to learn, but also an institution for getting men from A to Z to learn together and live together; and the living together cannot be achieved through correspondence courses, though grammar and geography can.

Here we seem to find the clearest case of all for a 'common good'. Yet even here we must insert our safeguards. There need in these cases be no 'community'. Wherever A and B trust each other, C and D show mutual sympathy, E and F co-operate, these states of affairs are all intrinsically good. So 'common good' (if it means the good of a community) is still a phrase with no application. It may well be true that the existence of an association, by providing a permanent basis for them, may heighten and diversify these good human relationships, yet the association is still only a means to the production of good.

I may now sum up the inroads made by this whole section on the theory that moral action is identical with service of the State.

(i) We first observed some elements of value in moral actions which had nothing to do with their consequences and therefore nothing to do with their value to the State. These were the motive and the amount of effort directed to doing right.

(ii) We then noticed that even when actions are aimed at consequences which are intrinsically good, these goods are sometimes non-social and therefore *a fortiori* non-political in character. Examples were truth, beauty and worship. In addition, when a 'common good' is sought, one of these non-social goods is usually the object, and its wider distribution is irrelevant to the non-social character of its goodness. 'Public health' was our example here.

(iii) We admitted that some goods, such as friendship, may be themselves intrinsically 'common' or social because they character-ise human relationships, but we insisted that they require no association for their manifestation. We rejected the attempt to devise an association to include them by treating all human beings as a unit and calling the unit 'Society'.

(iv) Even when an association does assist in the achievement of individual good or embody social good, the association need not be the State.

(v) Following the hints suggested above, we analysed further the notion of 'common good' and found that the phrase is never literally significant, that no association has a good of its own, that associations are means to ends which could usually be other-wise achieved. We admitted that in some cases an association (or even, in particular, the State) is a better means than others and in some cases a necessary means to certain ends. But the ends were still intrinsically non-political.

(vi) We admitted finally that there were two special cases where 'common good' seemed applicable, (a) to describe service rendered to particular people because they were members of the agent's own association, and (b) to signify those goods which are intrinsically social such as friendship. But we recalled the points made above: that, with reference to the first, the association need not be a State; and for the second there need be no association at all.

How then does the value of the State and the call to her service come out of the above attack? (a) The State is an association. It is useful for achieving some ends and necessary for achieving others. What are these ends? (b) I may have special obligations to other men as members of my State which I should not have to non-members. These obligations may conflict both with my obligations to other men as men and with my obligations to members of other associations to which I belong. What relations of priority should hold between these obligations? (c) The State may on occasion provide an example of that enjoyed co-operation and conscious trust and sympathy which is intrinsically good. But other associations may also provide examples of this, and some human beings may achieve these relationships without having membership of any association in common. How far can the State expect to achieve these goods? To the questions raised in these three fields we must now turn.

(C)
The place of the State

10

THE STATE AS A CENTRE OF
SYMPATHY AND CO-OPERATION

The whole of the previous section (B) raised difficulties in the notion of State service as the moral ideal. We shall now consider, in view of these criticisms, how much the State can legitimately attempt to do. This will be treated under four heads:

    (i) The State as a centre of sympathy and co-operation.
    (ii) The ends for which political organisation is necessary or desirable.
    (iii) The relations between the State and other associations.
    (iv) The relations between the State and other States.

It will be shown that conclusions (iii) and (iv) are dependent on the conclusions of (ii). The whole of this section will inevitably be concerned with ideals and not with actualities, except so far as actual conditions illustrate essential principles. If the sections are thought of as discussing 'what any government can do or ought to do', rather than as sketching 'an ideal State', initial prejudices may perhaps be avoided.

It was argued above that sympathy and willing co-operation, wherever they are found, are intrinsically good. In this chapter it is considered how far the State can achieve these ends. Its obvious handicap is one of size. A family or a committee or a couple of friends are likely vehicles for these values, but it would seem impossible to expect that a whole State should ever achieve them. Nor indeed is any approximation to this commonly observable except in war. Under war conditions it does happen that men

help each other as fellow-citizens, that they feel that they are
engaged on a single task, and that, in the face of that task, individual self-seeking and local or petty ambitions are swept away.
Wherever this happens, it is good. Even in war, however, this
goal is too high for common humanity. These ideals of service
and fellowship are never felt by more than a part of the population, and even in them seldom survive the early moments or the
crisis of a war, before the inevitable disillusion sets in. *Disenchantment* by C. E. Montague is a brilliant study of the way in which,
in the War of 1914–18, this spirit swept across a nation, and
also of the ways by which it was swiftly and brutally destroyed.
'Most of those volunteers of the prime were men of handsome
and boundless illusions. Each of them quite seriously thought of
himself as a molecule in the body of a nation that was really, and
not just figuratively, "straining every nerve" to discharge an
obligation of honour. Honestly, there was as little about them as
there could humanly be of the coxcombry of self-devotion. They
only felt they had got themselves happily placed on a rope at
which everyone else, in some way or other, was tugging his best
as well as they.'[1] This is how the book opens, and the following
quotation comes from its close describing those same volunteers.
'For them Bellona has not the mystical charm, as of grapes out
of reach, which she had for the Henleys and Stevensons. All the
veiled-mistress business is off. Battles have no aureoles now in the
sight of young men as they had for the British prelate who wrote
that old poem about the "red rain"[2]. . . . They have seen trenches
full of gassed men, and the queue of their friends at the brothel-
door in Bethune. At the heart of the magical rose was seated an
earwig.'[3] The book between these two passages leads with a sense
of fatal inevitability from the one to the other. We can see how
the change came, how war brought out the worst everywhere, in
the Church,[4] the Press,[5] the Government, the Army, how even

1. P. 2.   2. Virtue grows 'watered by war's red rain'.   3. P. 219.
    4. For instance, the most popular of the Bishops commended the *King
Stephen* for sailing past a wrecked Zeppelin crew, struggling in the water and
calling for help, without rescuing them. This of course is a mild example of
what the pulpit provided. I quote it as the utterance of high authority.
    5. For instance, the most popular war correspondent wrote in the *Daily
Chronicle* on 30 July 1915: 'How we laughed the other day at a tale of the
Germans in some dug-outs when a number of grenades flung by skilful hands
caught them straight in their fat stomachs and blew them to bits! It was a rich
joke. . . . We laughed and laughed. . . . The killing of Germans is to them
[the British Tommies] no more than the killing of vermin. The more the
merrier.' Again a mild example, quoted because of the eminence of the author.

where decency lurked, in the trenches for instance, it was a soured and acid decency, the dogged acceptance of necessary evil rather than the high heroism of the early days, a determination to survive and defeat as much the inefficiency and corruption behind as the enemy in front. These examples have been taken from the first World War. In the second there were found neither the initial idealism nor, to anything like the same degree, the resultant disillusion and hysteria. But the 'Dunkirk spirit' in this country and the remarkable achievements of the Soviet forces illustrate the power of imminent danger to unify a people.

If it is true that the achievement of nation-wide solidarity of feeling and purpose requires war, and if even in war it is liable to be swiftly destroyed by inevitable reaction, then surely the price is too heavy, and we had better look, for centres of sympathy and co-operation, to small and non-political units such as families, laboratories, farms or friends.

It may be said, however, that the totalitarian States at first achieved something of this spirit without war. But even in them it required crises not unlike war (such as the imposition of sanctions on Italy) to bring about any powerful manifestation of national unity. In any case this was achieved only at a cost. It required that every human relationship should be linked to the national ideal. Women must bear children for the State; children must be educated for the State; workers must make steel for the State; religion must admit an overriding loyalty to the State. Even when all this succeeds, there is a certain artificiality in the result. It is only by endless pressure and propaganda that the note can be sustained. A trivial instance will show what I mean. A young Dutchman whom I met on the Rhine in 1936 spoke to me sadly about the youth hostels there. Before the Nazi régime he had walked along this route and made many friends. In every hostel boys and girls made stews or music or love as they felt inclined. After the Nazis came to power, he said, he made no friends. A hostel would be empty for six days and on the seventh would be packed full by a company of Hitler Jugend, marching in a column under a leader, addressed on arrival by the village SA man, officially welcomed by the town band, officially responding with their own. He admitted that they seemed happy and keen, but, he added, 'too busy being German to have time to be human'.

This spirit of nation-wide loyalty and solidarity must be clearly distinguished from the spirit of co-operation which binds together a special group of men even when the group is serving the State, a cabinet or the officers of a battalion for example. In these cases the unit of co-operation is not the State as a whole, and genuine public service is compatible with a strong political or aristocratic or military caste feeling, which would make the soldier or the nobleman or the statesman incapable of the same sympathetic co-operation with his fellow-citizens outside his group. C. E. Montague again illustrates the opposite spirit. 'Little, white, prim clerks from Putney—men whose souls were saturated with the consciousness of class—would abdicate freely and wholeheartedly their sense of the wide, unplumbed, estranging seas that ought to roar between themselves and Covent Garden Market porters'.[1] The Boer War, which was waged by a professional army against a citizen army, provided a good illustration of this contrast. I do not believe that even the supporters of the war-policy in Britain ever felt that they were bound together as fellow-workers in a single national endeavour, as the Boers did. The test is whether a soldier feels that he is first and foremost a soldier defending civilians, or that he is a citizen fighting in an army.

Thus a definite group of men may achieve good results for their fellow-citizens, and (within their own group) the special good result of fellowship and sympathy, and this without any of the dangers consequent on the attempt to achieve fellowship and sympathy on the national scale. For fellowship between men seeing each other every day and working visibly together is a natural growth, whereas the national feeling requires an artificial stimulus.

On the whole, then, political theory should reject unity of national feeling as one of the goods at which political organisation should aim. It is too expensive to be justified. Yet when we cast up the accounts we must not leave it out. We must remember that war may achieve this special good; it is a good, however, which can be achieved more safely and more naturally in units other than the State, without the sacrifices and dangers which the State expression of it entails. (Some other methods of achieving such a spirit of State unity are dealt with in a later chapter[2] where the present conclusion is sustained.) We must also remember that 'loyalty' in this sense is wrongly limited to national loyalty; for national loyalty is only a striking example of a spirit which has many other examples more permanently satisfying and more morally sound.

1. *Disenchantment*, p. 7.   2. Ch. 15.

I I

THE ENDS FOR WHICH
POLITICAL ORGANISATION IS
NECESSARY OR DESIRABLE

The present section applies in detail the results of section (B). It accepts therefore, as already established, the following points: (i) That the State is an association and that there are associations of other types; (ii) that the State, like all associations, must subserve ends beyond its own existence; (iii) that sacrifices for the State are defensible only if they are sacrifices for the ends for which the State exists; (iv) that all these ends involve individual human experience; (v) and that therefore sacrifice for the State is never morally right unless in this connection some person or persons are assisted to achieve something of intrinsic value.

I am taking a State to be an association distinguished by (a) territorial limits, (b) inclusiveness within these limits, (c) the power in its officers to exercise force and the fear of force as instruments of policy, and (d) the possession by its officers of ultimate legal authority. The last of these attributes may seem to be a corollary or merely a restatement of the third, but it seems to be an addition necessary in order to exclude the case of temporary domination by terror without any organised authority. We should not call the temporary terrorism of some local brigand or war-lord a 'State'. The existence of law (whether regarded as the instrument of the ruler's will or as applied by him) seems to be essential; and this in its turn involves some permanence and organisation. Nazi Germany, though it was a system based on terror, was a State. For there was an operative legal system even though it was regarded as an instrument of Hitler's will and subject to caprice in its application. As for the first two criteria,

D

which might also appear identical, the addition of (b) is rendered
necessary by examples such as a Church with territorial limits
which is yet not inclusive within them.

Our questions now become clearer. What ends require for their
achievement the organisation of men by reason of their domicile
rather than on any other basis? What ends are attainable only,
or most effectively, by law supported ultimately, if need be, by
force?

The ends of political organisation

1. *Security*. The first end achieved by the State is security of
life. We need only recall the lesson we learned from Hobbes.
To maintain that human life is intrinsically good, or 'sacred',
takes too easily perhaps the fences of suicide and euthanasia, but
at any rate life is essential for the other goods we recognise, and
the taking of the life of another against his will and for a private
end is sufficiently generally deemed evil. As Hobbes also saw, the
indirect consequence of unrestricted killing is a second and inevitable evil—fear. It is bad in itself and it makes all good activities impossible. The point here is that, until no man ever
harbours intentions against another's life, some provision against
homicide and its consequent terrors will be needed. Private enterprise will not avail, nor will the services of any society other than
the State. For the danger must be dealt with wherever it occurs,
and the association which deals with it must be inclusive. Moreover, the threat is ultimately a threat of force, and only by force
can it finally be met and conquered. No doubt some dangers to
life and many fears come from beyond our frontiers, and we shall
have to examine in a later chapter[1] the view that the State is
irrationally small considering this one of its purposes. But here
we need make only two observations. The principle of State control is right. The Nation-State is the largest unit now available,
and its supersession by a more inclusive unit, still exercising
force, would not alter the principle. A World-State would still
be a State. On a smaller scale we can see that these functions of
the State were not altered when England and Wales or England
and Scotland were united. At present we patch up the situation,
so far as private dangers are concerned, by extradition treaties.
But, of course, one of the greatest dangers to our lives and the
most justifiable source of fear is war. Against that danger too the
State must take precautions, even though it seems that its own

1. Ch. 13.

existence as a unit creates the very danger it tries to avoid. This paradox (and the allied paradox of having to seek security by armament races which make the danger even more appalling) we must also leave to a later chapter.[1]

2. *Social conduct.* There are wrongs other than murder from which (and from the fear of which) men may legitimately claim to be protected. The State maintains, by force and fear if necessary, a general level of external conduct between man and man. This is the purpose of criminal law. There are alternative methods of trying to achieve this end. A government might attempt to standardise certain modes of action by means of advice. It might proclaim that citizens are 'requested to follow' this or that procedure. (Compare the employment of 'courtesy cops' on the roads.) Or again it might decide to deal with each case as it arose in the manner most effective for the common welfare. Anarchists have wavered between these alternatives and a third—that of doing nothing to enforce a standard of behaviour but merely giving arbitrational decisions between conflicting parties, decisions binding only by consent. Law has the advantage of making behaviour more predictable. Its threats may be so effective as to make punishments unnecessary. It promises to the good citizen a certain minimum of security in his life.

3. *Settlement of disputes.* In the life of any body of men there are inevitably honest disagreements as well as attempts at cheating, and the former may require as a last resort impartial settlement. This is the sphere of civil law. Once again the unit which is to impose such decisions must be both inclusive and compulsory if it is to achieve its object. Law is not the only conceivable method, and here one alternative, arbitration, has had a genuine trial; but, as before, the advantages of law are manifest. If I know my liabilities in advance I can plan my course of action more effectively than I could if each difficulty had to be settled by an isolated fiat. Whether law or arbitration is adopted, the State must be our unit. Only an inclusive body has the status necessary for settling disputes. Here again, however, the State, as it exists, is not inclusive enough. Economic relations are now so completely international that it is only by means of a collection of myths and fictions that we keep any appearance of State control and avoid the logical reference to a Hague Court or some other really inclusive authority. Institutions operating as the Postal Union did are the beginnings of genuine international economic control. It

1. Ch. 13.

must again be noted, however, that even if the Nation-State is too small a unit for the effective administration of civil law, this will not remove civil law from State control, but only set the boundary of the State wider.

There might seem to be a solution in separating civil from criminal law and moving swiftly towards an international civil code and international economic control, leaving criminal law to lag behind in national units until the wireless, the cinema and the great empires have finally denationalised moral standards. But this separation is not really practicable. The civil and the criminal codes are too closely intertwined. Perjury, false pretences, conspiracy and fraud arise in civil cases; and, in many criminal cases, questions of damages are inevitably raised. Further, as is all too obvious at present, the economic life and interests of a nation cannot be separated from its moral or cultural interests; nor, therefore, can they ever come under effective international jurisdiction so long as the nation is retained as the final authority in these other fields.

4. *Other purposes*. The method adopted in the preceding paragraphs was to point to a human need, to consider the possible methods of satisfying it, and to maintain that the only or the best method required the operation of an inclusive and compulsory unit.

Now the ends achieved by criminal and civil law are in a sense 'second-order' ends, for they presuppose other ends and secure men in their unimpeded pursuit of these. But there may be ends which men pursue directly, in the achievement of which the State may be concerned. In looking for these ends I can see no unifying principle among them and no system or scheme to which they must belong. The examples I shall take are therefore only examples. Each must be dealt with on its merits and in isolation, and others may be added, if it is found that they fulfil the necessary conditions. In each case, however, the method of argument is in principle the same.

(*a*) *Health*. I take it without argument that disease is evil and health is good. Until recently health was not a State concern. Each man pursued it for himself. He could get a doctor to help him, if he could afford it. He could combine voluntarily with other individuals for treatment or exercise, if he could afford it. Voluntary societies, from charitable or benevolent motives, might help to bring health to those who had not got it and could not afford to pay. Why did the State suddenly enter this field? It was not merely that some people were too poor to afford doctors and, unaided by any benevolent association, were neglected and diseased. This might have justified greater activity by the benevolent and its extension on non-sectarian lines to all deserving cases, but it would not have made health *necessarily* a State concern. It was not merely that the cash nexus gave the whole medical profession an interest, not in keeping people well, but in keeping them ill, with the inevitable evils of unnecessary operations, treatment determined by the patient's purse and so on. This might have been met by rising standards of professional conduct, and an extension of the readiness, already widely found in country practices, to do good work for the poor for little or nothing.

No doubt these methods could never have entirely removed the abuses nor given the poor any real chance of efficient attention or adequate treatment. But there was one factor which made State action in medicine more than an attempt to protect the rich hypochondriac from exploitation or the poor patient from neglect and inefficiency. This factor was the germ theory of disease, with the consequent recognition that no man can by his own efforts achieve health in an unhealthy community, that my own health is endangered unless my neighbour is compelled to keep his premises sanitary and to isolate his infectious cases. It is endangered also if those things which I cannot supply for myself—gas, water and roads—are not kept clean. Just as no individual and no voluntary association can prevent murder and insecurity, so neither of these can control the incidence of plague or typhoid or diphtheria. Freedom from disease can be achieved only by State action. The methods to be adopted must be judged by practical evidence and are no concern of political philosophy.

Three of the possible methods have already been tried in this country: (i) control of private persons (doctors and patients) by regulation, as in the case of infectious disease; (ii) the working of private persons (doctors and patients) into a national system, as with the Insurance Acts; and (iii) the employment of State doctors, as with the Medical Officer of Health. The relative merits of these three methods, the division of the care of health between them, and the proper development of any one at the expense of the others cannot be determined by any theoretical discussion. All that political theory can do is to lay bare the necessary connection between the germ theory and State action, and to leave detailed application to statesmen and scientists.

In the above discussion I have to some extent confused the

issue by treating 'health' and 'freedom from disease' as equivalent terms. Recent developments in this country have brought out very clearly that there is here a distinction of principle. Has the State a duty to promote health in a positive way as well as to prevent disease? This seems to me far less certain. The duty of the State would seem here to rest on the fact that, unless facilities for the positive pursuit of health are State-provided, some people will have no access to them at all (whereas in the case of infectious disease, unless State action is taken, not only some but all citizens are threatened). There are arguments by which the interest of all in the positive health of some might be defended. It is obviously to my interest that my poor neighbour should not have typhoid. Is it to my interest that my poor neighbour should have a playing-field, which I shall not use but for which I shall pay? It may be said that I may want my poor neighbour to fight for me, or with me, for my home, and that he will fight better if he is fit. This has no doubt been a powerful motive in countries whose governments have regarded war as desirable, or as the main objective of national organisation. But anyone who regarded war as a necessary evil would have to regard any expenditure on physical fitness, incurred with this ultimate object only, as a necessary evil also. This 'security' argument is therefore inadequate.

It may be said that my neighbour will be less cost to me if he has his playing-field than if he does not. For he will be more fit and the other work of the public health authorities will be lessened and made less expensive. But once again I think the ordinary man would feel that this was a sophism and would not expect his contribution to public health to diminish in proportion to his increased contribution to national fitness. For he knows that the enemy is so vast and so insidious that no gain in one place would really justify retrenchment in another. This 'economy' argument is therefore inadequate also.

But if these arguments are immoral, like the war argument, or sophistical, like its alternatives, there is nothing left to which we can appeal but the simple principles of benevolence or justice. Yet why should the exercise of these virtues be State-organised or made compulsory by an addition to our rates or taxes? Why should benevolence or justice be exercised on behalf of our fellow-citizens in particular? The answer to the latter question is that, while justice and benevolence should not be so limited, our fellow-citizens have a prior claim upon us, on the principle defended above that membership of an association creates claims on the members. The virtues themselves should be State-organised or made compulsory because this is the only effective way of exercising them in the cases in question. These arguments are all relevant to another case considered below, that of education.

(*b*) *Roads.* The gradual development of State control and State upkeep of roads is another clear instance of the general principle. It has replaced a chaos of local control, tolls, turn-pikes, private roads, estate roads, etc. The factor which corresponded to the germ theory in making State control inevitable was the internal combustion engine. When travel and transport on the roads are reckoned in hundreds of miles a day it is futile to make each individual repair his own frontage of road or to leave sections of road under private control. It is hardly more reasonable to leave local authorities to cope with their own roads unaided. Cyclists of twenty years ago will remember the jolt with which they passed from Perthshire (a relatively rich county) to Argyllshire (a poor county). The falsity of the county principle, that only Argyllshire dwellers use the Glencoe road, has justified the great new highway there; and what is true of Glencoe is even truer of Stamford or Oxford, through which the big lorries thunder all night. Once again, only an inclusive unit with compulsory powers can give the people what they need.

(*c*) *Education.* In a small Scottish town of three thousand inhabitants there were in 1850 fifteen schools, and a substantial proportion of the children attended none of them. There are now two schools, one primary and one secondary, and all the children go to one or the other. This is typical of all Scotland, and, though social distinctions have made the rate of change slower in England, all change is in this direction there also. The case of State education is first that without it some children would receive no education at all. The arguments above on health are all relevant here. The germ theory and the motor car have their parallel. What makes education in this country not merely a measure of benevolence and justice, but also something of genuine national importance, is the introduction of universal franchise. Besides these values there may be added the merits, even for those who would anyhow have received education, of State supervision. In the old days of private schools teachers were often unqualified and many of them taught in conditions which would render even a qualified teacher impotent. Parents are not usually educational experts and cannot be expected to know all about educational needs, nor might they choose with wise discrimination if they did. It is interesting to see how even schools which need not do so welcome visits and reports from the Inspectors of the Ministry of Education as a way of checking their own efficiency. There is no need for complacency about our system, but no one who knows what it has replaced and is replacing can have any doubts about the advance which has been made, an advance made possible only by State control.

Here, then, are three examples of State action where a clear case can be made out. No doubt each field has its dangers. So long as State and nation coincide and the spirit of nationalism grips the State machinery all three activities may be abused. National health may then be merely a cloak for military training; national roads may be merely strategic routes; and national education the implanting of racial hatred and national pride. But these abuses are not inevitable and on the whole the great democracies have avoided them.

5. *Economic action in relation to individuals.* In this and the following section the issue of Socialism must be raised. The claim of Socialism is that, despite all our discussion of political liberty and legal equality, no real liberty or equality is possible so long as individual incomes show great disparity and economic power can be used to direct the lives of men in the interests of those who possess the power. The interest of political theory in this problem turns on the cures which are proposed. These are notoriously various. Some would require the State to redistribute and equalise private incomes; some would support State ownership and the nationalisation of production and distribution; others, like the orthodox communists, would hold that the State is the tool of those who have vested interest in the maintenance of inequality and that it is therefore absurd to look to the State for remedies. It must disappear in a revolution and be replaced by a system controlled 'from below' by voluntary organisation of the workers and not 'from above'.

Firstly, against the orthodox Marxist, who says that 'political authority is the official expression of class antagonism'[1] or that 'with the disappearance of classes the State too will disappear and be relegated to the museum of antiquities along with the spinning-wheel and the bronze axe'[2] because 'the State is the sanction of triumphant force and brutal inequality',[3] I would repeat the conclusions reached above. Criminal law, civil law, health, transport communications, education—all these require political organi-

1. Marx.   2. Engels.   3. Bukharin.

sation and political authority. If the State 'withers away', then
health, education, security and justice will wither away too, and it
will be seen that it is Marxism which belongs to the museum along
with the bronze axe. Of course, if by 'State' is meant only those
activities of any government which are directed towards oppression and the maintenance of economic inequality, then the
question is one of words. But an honest examination of legislation
passed through the British Parliament since 1865 accompanied
by the question, after each law, 'Would the disappearance of
classes have made this law unnecessary?' should convince the most
bigoted Marxist (if the example of present-day Russia did not
convince him) that his aim is really more State action and not the
disappearance of State action altogether.

Secondly, money is a means, not an end. The fundamental issue
is not an economic one, and the orthodoxy which makes economic
pressure ultimate rests on a fiction as dangerous as the fictions
of rank or title. Values—'goods and services' in the widest sense
—are the issue. Should the State concern itself with these? Once
again, only the most general conclusions are possible in such a
work as this. What is to be done about those who cannot support
themselves—the old, the infirm, children, the unemployed? The
alternatives are clear and exhaustive. Either we must disown all
responsibility for them or we must recognise the need of State
aid. Why *State* aid? Why should not religious bodies, trade
unions, charitable societies and kindly individuals take up these
burdens? As before, the answer is that the State is exclusive. If
help is to be given to starving men (and not merely to starving
Baptists or starving boiler-makers) the State alone has the
necessary status and the necessary power. (I do not see how this
can be treated as a question of 'rights'. I do not think a man has
a 'right' to be given work or food or medicine or a house by the
State. Similarly, I think that, if I overtake a weary traveller, I
ought to give him a lift in my car, though I should not say he has
a right to it. As I attempted to show above, rights are derivative and
not ultimate and they derive in the end from goods or evils, which
are procured or avoided by the maintenance of a rule or an
institution. But here the good is no indirect consequence of a
rule or institution. An evil exists; a good is lacking. The evil can
be removed or the good procured only by State action. Let the
State therefore act.)

But should the State go further? This question cannot be
answered by the political theorist, for (except where State action

is *necessary* as in the above instances, to achieve a good) the State stands on a level with other associations and with individuals as a competitor. *Only* the State can secure health and education and support for the old or infirm. But whether nationalisation or syndicalism or sovietism or equalisation of incomes or private enterprise will give the individual more good and less evil (not necessarily more money) can only be decided by economic analysis and historical enquiry, by sociology and empirical psychology. This problem is therefore no part of political philosophy. I see no *general* reason why any one system should be right and the others wrong.

6. *Economic action in relation to industries.* Besides the possibility of State action in relation to individual incomes there is also the general question of its relation to industry as a whole. What should the State do about agriculture, mining, the milk trade, etc? *Laissez faire* (except for health regulations), nationalisation, compulsory rationalisation, national marketing, subsidies—these are all possible governmental attitudes. Again I do not think the political philosopher competent to choose between them. There seems to me no theoretical reason why any particular solution should be right for one industry, much less for all industries. If certain agricultural products are best produced at home (or must be produced at home in war-time and war is probable), or if the retention of some of the population on the land is desirable, and if (owing to foreign competition or dumping) this home production is economically impossible, then there is a case for State action. But each of these 'ifs' can only be made a 'because' by enquiry into the facts. And even if the facts justify State action, that rules out only *laissez faire* from our list and leaves all the other possibilities open; and the choice between them cannot be made on theoretical gounds but must be based on factual enquiry. In industry therefore I find no *a priori* grounds for State action, but only a claim which must rest on the facts in each case, where these suggest that some action is necessary and that State action would succeed.

'Planning' and State action. I said above that the relief of unemployment is a State responsibility. But it is obviously better that unemployment should be prevented than that it should be 'relieved' by doles, etc. If the 'Keynesian' analysis is correct, *laissez-faire* individualism can never prevent mass-unemployment, and the only remedy is a comprehensive socialisation of investment. There are other factors, too—shortages or maldistribution

of materials, over-production, the tariff policies of other States—which may require interference with the free play of economic processes. Many of these difficulties could be rationally solved only by economic action on a world scale, and the first attempts to solve them on this scale are now being worked out. But as things stand such world arrangements can be the result only of voluntary agreement. The State is the only body, at the present stage of our development, which can lay down and enforce any planned system of investment, capital supply, distribution, or production. Once again the fields and the degrees in which such State action is desirable or necessary must be determined in each case by empirical enquiry. The aim of a sound political philosophy in this field would be to avoid any *a priori* judgments. Controls should neither be removed wholesale at the bidding of a doctrinaire individualism nor be imposed wholesale at the bidding of a doctrinaire socialism.

12

THE STATE AND OTHER ASSOCIATIONS

We have noticed above that much of what Rousseau and Hegel
say about the State applies to any association. The theory of the
common good and the general will, the idea of the unity of a
group co-operating for a common purpose, and the psychological
facts of corporate loyalty and sympathy—all these have no
special *political* reference. As soon as this is observed, the problem
of the relations between different associations becomes unavoidable. It is a problem which in its general form is peculiar to
modern political theory. The traditional resistance to Hegelian
theory and practice came, as we have seen, from the side of the
individual and pleaded rights and liberties of individuals in
opposition to political absolutism. In practice the individual has
little power against the modern State, but associations such as
Churches and trade unions cannot be so easily overridden. In
theory also a new movement has arisen, to which the name
'Political Pluralism' has been given (though 'Social Pluralism'
would have been less misleading, since the many units which this
theory substitutes for the State are not political units). This
'pluralist' position has been maintained by such writers as the
Guild Socialists in England and the Syndicalists in France. The
position is that the error of the Hegelian theory was not its belief
in the importance of the general will and of corporate unity but
in looking for this will and unity to the State alone.

I shall state the four possible views of the relation between the
State and other associations, then sketch the recent history of
these relations in England as an illustration of the importance of

theory in practice, and then finally consider in turn the four views and attempts to assess their value.

The first theory of the relation of the State to other associations may be called Abstract Monism. It regards the existence of other associations as a sign that the State is lacking in unity, and its practical corollary is their suppression, by force if necessary. The second is Concrete Monism. It admits the value of functional associations but regards them as parts of the State, and its practical outcome is complete State control of their constitution and activities. The third view admits the necessity of the other associations and regards the State as a particular association with no superior value or status. The fourth maintains the need of associations with special functions but can find no special function for the State. Its practical application would be the abolition of the State and the transfer of all its functions to other associations.

I shall preface the consideration of these theories in detail by a brief sketch of the history of the position of trade unions in England, with some parallels from the position of religious bodies.

The State and trade unions: history of their relations in Britain.[1] Before the Industrial Revolution, control of wages and working conditions was supposed to be exercised directly by the State. Wages were to be fixed by statute or by the justices, who should 'call to them such discreet and grave persons as they think meet'[2] to help them in this work. The last recorded instance of this control occurred in 1726 when the weavers petitioned the King, and the Privy Council in settling the case admonished them 'always to lay their grievances in a regular way before the King, who would always be ready to grant them relief suitable to the justice of their case'.

The disappearance of this State control was due to the following factors: (i) the growth of industrial wealth driving together the industrialist and the landowner; (ii) the violent reaction of the workers against the introduction of machinery, which lost them the sympathy of the Government; (iii) the political and economic theory of *laissez faire*. This doctrine, developed by Adam Smith from the individualism of Locke, led to the conclusion that any attempt to fix wages was economically unsound, and therefore an 'act in restraint of trade' and consequently an infringement of Magna Charta. The results of *laissez faire* in the indus-

1. I owe the detail of this section to the works of S. and B. Webb and C. M. Lloyd on trade union history.
2. 1563.

trial field are well known and only a few instances need be cited. In Leeds, children worked a seventy-eight-hour week; Dundee mills employed ten-year-olds for fourteen hours a day; in the mines children began work at five years of age, doing jobs from the worst abuses of which pit ponies were later protected. Against these conditions workmen began to combine, and the resultant trade unions presented a serious problem to the Government, whose successive attempts to deal with it we shall now examine.

Suppression. The Combination Laws of 1799 and 1800 held that a trade union was a criminal conspiracy. Not only striking but any combined action was illegal. In 1800 Justices of the Peace could and did give up to two months' hard labour for joining with other workmen for any purpose whatsoever. Yet the unions grew apace, for the police were few and ineffective, and workmen were prosecuted only under pressure from an individual employer. In 1824 the Combination Laws were repealed, but in 1825 re-enacted with the exception that meeting and consultation were no longer crimes. The strike, the workman's only protection against the employer's weapon of dismissal, was still illegal. Lord Jeffreys pointed out that employers were also subject to Combination Laws, but employers have no need to combine if workmen may not do so, and in fact no case of prosecution of employers is recorded between 1800 and 1825, though hundreds of cases occurred involving workmen. Here at once we see the inconsistency of the legal position. A workman may give up his work (Statute of Labourers); a number of workmen is a mere aggregate and not a new entity in the eyes of the law, yet a number of workmen may not simultaneously give up their work. The attack on the unions continued during the next fifty years. The best-known case was that of six labourers of Tolpuddle who committed the crime of binding themselves by oath to attempt to get their wages raised from seven shillings to ten shillings a week. Their sentence of seven years' deportation was, however, soon remitted owing to public protests.

Towards non-recognition. By 1871 the attempt to suppress trade unions had failed so completely as to be ludicrous. The land was full of these vast 'criminal conspiracies'. So in 1871 and 1876 laws were passed making them no longer criminal. Corporate action and consultation could no longer be punished by imprisonment or deportation. But this attempt at non-recognition produced its own absurdities and injustices. Trade unions, being legally non-existent, could not make contracts, hold property, or appear at law. Their property had therefore to be deemed to belong to their officials. When the officials embezzled it they were consequently acquitted. Some judges in their decisions encouraged this embezzlement by assuring officials of their legal impunity. Then the old false logic crept back in a new guise. The unions, no longer criminal conspiracies, were treated as civil conspiracies. Strikers could not be imprisoned by the Government for striking but they could be successfully prosecuted for damages by the employers concerned. Even this illogical procedure was administered with partisan bias, as may be seen by comparing the Mogul Shipping Case with the Belfast Butcher-boys' Case. In the former (1892) a shipping ring boycotted a non-member. He sued them for damages as being a civil conspiracy. The pure logic triumphed. What one could do, all could do; the 'ring' had no legal existence; the plaintiff got no damages. In the Belfast case (1901) the Union of Butcher-boys persuaded two of its members to refuse to work for a low-wage employer. In this case the employer got his damages and the union leaders were bankrupted. This result raised the problem of funds. The Belfast Union had no funds and the bankruptcy of individual butcher-boys cannot have been very satisfying.

What was wanted was a decision by which a union should be treated as a civil conspiracy when it persuaded its members to withdraw their labour, and simultaneously as a legal person holding property so that the property could be removed as damages. This was the triumph achieved by the Taff Vale Case (Taff Vale Railway Co. *v*. Amalgamated Society of Railway Servants, before the House of Lords, 1901)—perhaps the most curious perversion of justice in recent English legal history. Here was clearly a parting of the ways. One course was to recognise the trade unions and consequently to allow them all legal functions including the holding of property and the withdrawal of labour, but to hold them responsible for any wrongful actions (breach of contract, breach of the peace, etc.). The other and the logical course on the prevalent monistic legal theory was to regard the union as legally non-existent and consequently to make its funds unassailable and its officers exempt from prosecution.

Non-recognition. The Liberal Government of 1906 chose the latter course. The Trade Disputes Act (1906) says that 'An act done in pursuance of a combination or agreement by two or more persons shall, if done in contemplation or furtherance of a trade dispute, not be actionable, unless the act, if done without any such agreement or combination, would be actionable.' Here again is the logic of pure monism. Section 4 of the Act swept away the legal precedent created by the Taff Vale decision. It rendered the union funds unassailable by any action against officials for tort, except for some special cases. This section has caused much outcry among legal experts. Dicey calls it a 'triumph of legalised wrong-doing'.[1] But the alternative was to recognise trade unions and define their purposes. Only this could have enabled the law to hold the officials responsible for acts *ultra vires* and made their funds liable for tort.

The law had a further lapse when it once more fell back into its old attitude. The Osborne Judgement (1909) held that a levy by a trade union for a political purpose was *ultra vires*. This was equivalent to recognising and defining the purposes of the unions. This decision in its turn was wiped out as a precedent by the Act of 1913 which allowed the political levy with 'contracting out' by those who do not wish to subscribe. Finally, with the series of Health Insurance Acts the unions have become part of the working machinery of government.

The most recent judgment on this subject shows how far legal opinion has come since 1870. 'The legislation in question contained many specific examples of attributes of legal personality expressly attributed to trade unions; for example, the right to own property, nominally vested in trustees; the right to register, and change, an identifying name; and the right to bring or defend actions in the name of trustees.

'The quality of legal personality thus clearly attributed to trade unions necessarily connoted the general power to do at any rate many of the things inherent in the legal concept of personality. He [his Lordship] could see no *prima facie* ground for limiting by any implication the list of powers normally attendant on legal personality. The true interpretation of the Acts, in his opinion, was that a trade union was given all the powers of a *persona juridica* except those *solely* characteristic of a natural person and those expressly excepted by the creating or enabling statute.' (Court of Appeal, 25 October 1945.)

This whole history shows how such associations originate to meet a need, grow as their work succeeds, acquire functions, develop their own activities, become organised with constitutions of their own and property of their own, and resist successfully all attempts to destroy or crush them. If the State will not take the

1. *Law of the Constitution*, 8th ed., p. xi.

extreme course of suppressing them it is driven logically beyond its weaker alternative of non-recognition to face these facts. The development of the official attitude has been shown above. A trade union was successively (1) a criminal conspiracy (1799–1870), (2) a civil conspiracy (1870–1906), (3) a mere aggregate of men (1906–1909), (4) an association with a fixed and limited purpose (1909–1913), (5) an association with its own powers of self-control and development taking a positive place among the recognised institutions of the country (1913 onwards).

The State and Churches: history of their relations in Great Britain. The trade union is only one specimen of such associations. One theorist of the new revolt against Abstract Monism asks whether an association 'is to be conceived as possessing any living power of self-development or whether it is to be conceived either as a creature of the State or held rigidly under the trust-deeds of its foundation'.[1] He is speaking not of trade unions but of Churches; and, since the attitude of governments to the Unions may have been affected by class or party prejudice as well as by false legal and political theory, it is worth noticing that these same errors can be seen in the relations between Church and State in this country (where no class or party issue is involved). We can find suppression in the attacks on Catholics and the disabilities of dissenters before the Test Acts. We can see the attempt to treat a Church as a mere State department in the attempt to compel ministers of the Church of England to marry divorced persons. Till 1937 the law forced the minister to allow his church to be used for this purpose.[2] Our greatest legal authority thought we should return to the old demand that the minister should be compelled to officiate. 'A clergyman of the Church of England is an official of the National Church yet while acting as an official of the State he is virtually allowed to pronounce immoral a marriage permitted by the morality of the State.'[3] We have seen the State dictation again more recently in the rejection by Parliament of the Revised Prayer Book. If it is supposed that this claim is made possible only by the fact of Establishment, we may notice first that the Scottish Church has

1. J. N. Figgis, *Churches in the Modern State*, p. 39. The notes which follow are derived mainly from this excellent and too little known book.

2. An incumbent could, however, 'supervise the ordering of the service'. By ordering the altar to be draped in crêpe, the bell to be tolled, and the organist to play the 'Dead March', he was usually able to keep the wedding civil.

3. Dicey, *Law and Public Opinion*, p. 315.

the Establishment without the interference, and secondly that the claim has not been limited by its upholders to Established Churches. 'I don't think it is in the power or duty or right of any Church to superadd its own conditions to what the law considers sufficient in the case of civil marriage.'[1] We may find the attempt to tie down a Church to its 'original purpose', an attempt comparable to the Osborne Judgment, in the Scottish Free. Church case. Here a split in the Church led to a dispute about the property. The Court of Appeal awarded the property to the small minority on the grounds that it was upholding the 'original doctrines' of the Church. This denial to the Church of a power to grow and develop had swiftly to be reversed because of the widespread revolt against it. But it shows the legal attitude clearly.

With these historical lessons in mind we may turn to a discussion of the central problem. We shall consider the theories in the order: (1) Abstract Monism, (2) Concrete Monism, (3) Pluralism. We shall show where each fails and then attempt to work out the fourth theory, that of the State as a specialised association among others.

Abstract monism. This is the theory that the State is the only association necessitated by the moral and psychological nature of man and that all others are to be prohibited or destroyed. Morally considered, the existence of various associations creates conflicts of duty for which there can be no solution. Psychologically it creates rival loyalties which render a stable and happy life impossible. These are the results for the individual, and if we look at the situation from the point of view of the State the same arguments are strengthened. The simile of the body which suffers from a parasitic internal growth is apt and expressive. Richard of Devizes called the rival association '*tumor plebis*'; Hobbes says the associations are 'like worms in the entrails of the natural man'. Rousseau expresses the position clearly and gives the arguments for it. 'When factions arise and partial associations are formed at the expense of the great association, the will of each of these associations becomes general in relation to its members while it remains particular in relation to the State. . . . It is therefore essential, if the general will is to be able to express itself, that there should be no partial society within the State.'[2] (The effect of this theory in French history was seen in 1792. 'The National Assem-

1. J. H. Campbell, Member for Dublin University (7 February 1911), speaking of the Roman Catholic Church.
2. *Contrat Social*, Book II, ch. 11.

bly, considering that a State which is truly free should not allow in her bosom any association, not even those which by their services to public education have deserved well of the nation, decrees as follows: The corporations known in France under the titles of congregations, secular and ecclesiastical . . . and generally all corporations whether religious or secular composed of men and women, clerical or lay . . . are annulled and suppressed from the date of the publication of the present decree.')

The arguments and the forces on the other side are well known but they must be briefly repeated. The psychological force against abstract monism is a force on which it itself relies, the natural co-operative sociability of man. But the difficulty is that, when his sociability takes its natural course, it does not make him a 'political animal'. For the State is too large for any man naturally to feel united with his fellow-citizens and his interests are too complex for him naturally to express them in a single society. The result is that the monistic State has artificially to propagate the notion of its own supreme unity and value. The second difficulty arises from the first. The State is compelled not only to suppress all associations within it but also to dominate all human activity. In regard to the various interests of human life it will oscillate between attempts to destroy and attempts to absorb them. Both attempts are doomed to failure.

Abstract Monism therefore is no solution to our problems. Its recent embodiments continued to exist only by the use of non-political worships such as those of a Hero or a Race (see below, Chapter 15). These worships involved the falsification of fact in an increasing degree. Both the worships themselves and the monistic attitude to all human interests and values involved the victimisation of the most courageous and independent citizens; they involved official adoption of aims and methods of which any decent citizen had to remain ignorant or be ashamed, they involved the progressive corruption of public and private life. For the continuance of the system there was required a supply of rulers who combined with a genius for demagogy either cynical effrontery and a lust for power or a maniacal belief in the objects for which the State was supposed to stand. This belief had to be maniacal, since it had to be held independently of all adverse evidence, because the leader could not always be protected, as the subjects might be, from the impact of such evidence.

Concrete monism. This is the theory which welcomes within the State associations of all types but attempts to make them part of the State machinery, subordinated to its needs and its officers in every particular. This Corporative State was the theoretical ideal of Fascism—though in practicè there was little difference between it and Nazism. This Concrete Monism was also the theory of Hegel in contrast to the Abstract Monism of Rousseau. The strength of such a system was claimed to lie in its efficiency. It tried to escape the personal feuds which go on behind the façade of an abstract monist State and within its dominant Party by departmentalising all its functions. It tried to create a machine with more chance of survival that an individual dictator had. The Government of such a State could claim allegiance not because it was mystically inspired nor because it was the voice of God or of race, but because it had created an organisation which was efficient and got things done.

The weakness of the Corporative State is its incompleteness and its compromise character. A corporative organisation with the Church outside it is obviously weakened at its roots. It is true, as we shall see later, that the more purely 'economic' an association is the more easily it can be absorbed by the State. But among the Italian corporations was included the Corporation of Art and the Professions; and, remembering that freedom is essential to art and science and philosophy, we can feel sure that so far as this corporation was active at all its action was destructive. The resolutions of the Syndicate of Professions and Artists (1936) affirmed that 'the organisations of professional men and artists represent in the corporative State that indispensable element of culture and technique in virtue of which the various elements of national production are integrated and reinforced. They collaborate to achieve the essential finality of the State itself. . . . And above all by the direct participation in the life of the State achieved as stated above the Corporation of Professions and Arts represent a force which will discipline and direct anew that activity which exhibits the highest manifestation of the spiritual life of Fascist Italy.'[1] Even with the economic associations the State cannot achieve its end of harnessing specialised associations to its purposes. For there also the genuine representation of special interests is incompatible with the State's control. This was noticeable when many different trades were compelled to join one corporation so that the number of corporations should not become unwieldy; it was noticed again in the control by the Fascist Party, which provided a president and secretary for each corporation.

1. *Le Corporazione nel Primo Anno di Vita* (Rome, 1936).

Everywhere was to be seen the contradiction inherent in the law by which corporations were first established. 'Syndical or professional organisation is *free*. But only the legally recognised syndicate, subjected to the control of the State, has the right to represent all the category of employers and employed.'[1] The position in Italy was complicated by the fact that in economic life private enterprise remained recognised as the ideal method of production, and so far as this was maintained it meant that much vital control fell outside the corporations altogether, and also that in any clash of interests those of the employer were likely to triumph over those of the workman or the consumer. The exceptions occurred only when the Government itself was moved by some abuse or danger or injustice to intervene and impose a wage-rate or other regulation, but this could hardly be regarded as a triumph of the corporative principle. The corporations were in fact mechanical, artificial and sterile. The only function they performed was that of keeping the Government informed about economic problems or conditions, the function performed by our unions when their officials give evidence before a Royal Commission. And they performed this function ineffectively, for they did not really represent the interests after which they were named, as officials of a free society elected by its members are at any rate more likely to do.

Pluralism. In revolt from all such monistic theories as those we have considered there have recently been movements called generally 'pluralist', though there is no complete agreement nor thorough-going logic among their supporters. Syndicalism and Guild Socialism are economic versions of the theory. Where the State Socialist said 'the mines for the Nation', the Syndicalist says 'the mines for the miners'. All functional associations are to be free and independent and together they will exhaust all the interests and loyalties of man. These theorists then ask, 'What does the State now do which a free functional association could not do better?' And their answer is, 'It makes war.' As a reaction against Abstract Monism this theory has had justifiable success. Against it, however, we need only recall our previous arguments on the functions of the State and apply their conclusions to associations as a special case. The idea that the State can 'wither away' and leave a pluralistic Society in its place[2] forgets all those necessities already defended. The protection of life, the maintenance of

1. Charter of Labour, Article 3.
2. This is the orthodox Marxist doctrine.

human relations effected by the criminal law, the settlement of disputes achieved by civil law, the accomplishment of those purposes which require to be organised on an inclusive, territorial basis—all these are functions which no civilised people can forgo and which no association other than the State can achieve. K. C. Hsiao in his book *Political Pluralism* has shown in detail how, when the 'pluralists' have tried to think out their proposals, they have had to admit the necessity of the activities enumerated above and have introduced into their systems institutions which are only the State under other names.

The State and other associations. Since neither of the extreme theories, Monism or Pluralism, really provides a tolerable solution of our problem, we turn to examine the possibility of fitting the essential elements of both into a single picture. The essential basis of such a picture is free association, on the grounds recognised above that, other things being equal, free human activity is good and that the consequences of freedom are also generally good. Freedom of association requires not only that no man shall be punished for founding or joining an association, but that, in default of any special reason to the contrary, an association once founded should be recognised as legally capable of holding property, making contracts, employing and being employed, buying and selling like any ordinary citizen. It should have the power of growth and change within a general continuity of membership and purposes.

These general claims for any association must be supplemented in special cases. For example, so far as the purposes of any association include any spiritual interest, its complete freedom from State interference is essential in respect to that interest.

The claims of the State in relation to individual subjects have already been worked out above and need only be applied to an association as to a special case. Every association in its corporate capacity must keep the peace, be subject to the criminal law, submit its disputes to the civil law, obey such regulations as are necessary for the achievement of those aims which only the State can secure, and contribute to the taxation which makes all the above State action possible.

There is one particular claim for freedom which associations have made which must be separately considered. It is parallel to the liberty of the individual claimed by Mill[1] for actions which concern himself alone. The claim is that the internal affairs of an

1. See above, p. 59–60.

association should never be liable to State interference. As the State deals with external relations of individuals, so it should be concerned with associations only when the action of an association involves another association or an individual who is not a member of the association in question. The implied result, that the State has no jurisdiction over the relations between an association and its own members, is sometimes supported by the argument that such associations are voluntary. No rigour in a monk's rule of life can be regarded as the basis for a claim that it is unjust or oppressive, since the monk voluntarily adopts it and can freely give it up. So it is held that the associations are voluntary in this sense, while the State is not. No one compels the member to join or to remain a member longer than he likes. There are therefore two questions. First, is the distinction between voluntary and compulsory associations valid, and are other associations voluntary and the State compulsory? Secondly, even if the other associations are voluntary, can they claim complete freedom in their internal affairs?

Voluntary and compulsory associations. A compulsory association may mean an association which it is literally impossible for a man to leave. In this respect States are seldom compulsory. 'Let him leave it if he does not like it' applies to the citizen of most countries. It is true, however, that the State is potentially compulsory in this sense, yet no more compulsory in regard to membership than in regard to anything else. It has the force to execute any command, provided that the command does not cause revolution. It is true also that States have refused passports and so made themselves arbiters of whether their inhabitants should be able to leave, and other States have excluded immigrants and thus created a further element of compulsion.

It may, however, be maintained that an association is compulsory if a member cannot leave it without considerable sacrifice. In a really powerful trade union a member can leave the Union if he does not mind changing the nature of his employment completely. This, however, is clearly a matter of degree. Even a Church may be far from voluntary in this sense, as inhabitants of Scottish or Welsh villages last century knew well. Indeed, if any society has a *raison d'être* at all it cannot be voluntary in this sense. The patron of a living appointing an incumbent might be tempted to argue that the churchmanship of a candidate is irrelevant, since those who do not like his practices can cease to attend; and this argument, while obviously unfair when applied to a village, might have some force in a town where there was a neighbouring church with a different practice. Yet even here it cannot be said that a member of a really living congregation can leave that congregation 'without sacrifice'. The difference is that in the town the sacrifice would not include a complete deprivation of corporate worship, as it would for the villager. Even with the most voluntary society therefore there is an element of loss in leaving it.

Freedom of internal affairs. I find no other ground on which complete freedom of action can be claimed for an association in relation to its members. Injustice and breach of faith may characterise these relations as easily as any others, and protection and appeal should here be equally possible. If an association penalises or expels a member without giving him a hearing, or if it victimises certain of its members on religious or political grounds when it is not itself a religious or political association, the member should be able to appeal and the State should intervene. No exception should be made here to those rules which the criminal and the civil law prescribe for the general relations between citizens. There was a case quoted by Figgis[1] in which a club raised its subscription. A member refused to pay and was expelled. He brought an action and the courts decided in his favour, holding that the club was bound by quasi-contractual obligations incurred at the time of that member's election. This decision is obviously unjust, yet the comments of Figgis in the context suggest that the club ought to be judge of its own needs and that the minority should have no right to appeal to the State. Suppose, however, that the proposal had been not to raise the general subscription but to raise to a prohibitive level the subscriptions of a certain class of members (say the country members or those elected before a certain date) so as to force their resignation; then not only would the members affected have a right to appeal but the State should in that case have found in their favour.

My conclusion therefore is that in all their relations associations should be under the control of the State in matters affected by the criminal and civil law and by the needs of peace and order, that they should also be subject to State regulation in connection with those ends which only State action can achieve, and that otherwise they should be free unless it can be shown in any particular case that State action achieves a certain end better than voluntary combination.

These general principles I shall next work out in two special

1. *Churches in the Modern State*, p. 65.

fields whose historical interest I considered above, the relations
between the State and trade unions and between the State and
the Churches.

The State and trade unions. The trade unions, as we have seen,
arose as associations of employed persons organised to achieve
a bargaining weapon against employers comparable to the weapon
of dismissal. It might therefore be thought that they are merely a
part of the working of a capitalist society, and that with the establishment of a classless society it would be the unions and not the
State which would wither away'.[1] The present functions of trade
unions in this country may be summarised as follows: (*a*) mutual
aid, (*b*) negotiation about wages and conditions of work, (*c*) co-
operation in productive activity, (*d*) disciplinary action against
their own members, (*e*) the administration of state insurance, (*f*)
political action by parliamentary representation, (*g*) striking.[2]
Of these seven functions the first four seem to be of permanent
value, whatever the Government of a country may be or do. The
fifth has developed naturally in this country where the Government recognised a duty in connection with unemployment some
time after the unions had already devised a working scheme of
insurance. There is no particular reason why the unions should
be involved, but the system has worked well in this country and
has made the unions an integral part of national economy—a far
cry from the attitude we observed between 1800 and 1906. The
sixth function is more doubtful. Indeed if representation is in
principle local, it is indefensible; and even when it is recognised
that representation is in fact party representation, parliamentary
action by trade unions is equally an anomaly, for the essence of
party representation is general agreement on principles and freedom of individual opinion on details, and Members of Parliament
who are tied to a specific non-party interest, whether they are
'brewers' M.P.s' or 'miners' M.P.s', are an anomaly. Even if the
Labour Party were explicitly a trade union party, the election to
Parliament of men to represent particular unions would be a
distortion of the party system. (A parallel distortion in the international field has recently appeared, when the World Trade
Union Conference claimed direct representation in the organisation of the United Nations.) The fact that trade union control
of M.P.s may still occur is due to three historical accidents: (*a*)
the nineteenth-century hostility of all governments to the trade
union movement, (*b*) the amateur character of English politics

1. See p. 105.   2. Ramsay Muir, *Trade Unionism*, ch. I.

which kept the M.P. unpaid until 1913 and also demanded largesse in the constituencies, with the result that the only large property-owners in the Labour ranks—the unions—had to pay the piper and therefore called the tune, (c) the late development of universal education, which meant that the few working men who had the opportunity and the personality to lead their unions were also practically the only men equipped to represent Labour in Parliament. All these three causes are now losing their influence and as a result union representation in Parliament is on the decline. But another field, and one almost equally important, is now open to the unions. Legislation based on Royal Commission reports is becoming a more and more effective method of achieving a genuinely democratic result, and union representation both on the commissions and among the witnesses is an essential feature in the preparation of any economic legislation.

The negative side of the activities of the unions we have already seen. No union shall break the peace or commit crimes or wrongs. Every union shall submit its disputes with other persons or bodies, including its own members, to the courts for settlement if necessary. As a property-owner, it shall keep its property in the condition which national health requires, and contribute through taxation towards the services necessary to achieve the legitimate ends of political organisation.

Strikes. The special feature of trade union action is the strike. We have shown above that the strike is a legitimate last resort against the employer's ultimate weapon, dismissal. But both strike and lockout are irrational methods of settling disputes and any improvement in the arbitrational machinery which will avert both of them is to be welcomed. The steelworkers, for instance, had no strikes between 1870 and 1920, and in 1924 ninety-seven per cent of the wage changes were negotiated without strikes.

The sympathetic strike. Some unions found that the recognition of their claims by the public or by the Government was a strong weapon against employers. But some strikes (such as a coal strike) operate so slowly in their effect on the consumer that this power was diminished. The miners could not fail to argue that the fact that the railwayman's wage increase after 1919 was thrice theirs had something to do with the speed with which a railway strike hits the public. Hence developed the sympathetic strike, in which unions with slow strike effect received the aid of unions with swift effect. This was the origin of the so-called 'General Strike' of 1926, which was not a general strike at all but a sympathetic strike involving the 'vital services'. Many observers would now disagree with the 'Astbury Judgment', which held that the strike was not 'in furtherance of a trade dispute'. No doubt a jury would have found against the strikers, but that is only because under such conditions, as in war, emotion conquers reason. There seems no legitimate ground for condemning the sympathetic strike as such, and Union leaders are not likely to countenance it unless considerable injustice is being done and widely resented.

Strikes in vital services. There is here another case for State action. There are certain services in which the operation of a strike is directly effective not against the employer but against the consumer; cases, moreover, in which the consumer is every citizen and his interest in the service one which touches his everyday life, so that it becomes completely disorganised by the withdrawal. Now the only body which can represent consumers is the State; and, when the threat to their working lives is such as we have described, the State is obliged to act. Where the threat is already in full action the State's first response must be to meet it and to maintain those services which it is the object of the strike to withdraw. In relation to these vital services in general, however, there are three prior possibilities. The first is legislation forbidding strikes in certain industries, the second is direct counter-action when the actual threat develops, and the third is the establishment of special machinery for the settlement of disputes in these industries. The first of these is already adopted in this country in connection with gas, water, electricity, police and merchant shipping. The second was prepared by the Emergency Powers Act, 1920, and was actually brought into effect in 1926. The third is a method recommended by a large body of employers and trade unionists in 1919 but forgotten in the boom which then followed the war. These proposals envisaged conciliation boards including not merely the disputing parties and the State but also representatives of other unions and employers' organisations, present in a consultative capacity. (This solution is strongly urged in *Industrial Conflict* by F. W. Ogilvie, to which I owe much of the above section. It should become increasingly important with the development of nationalisation.) This method has the advantage of strengthening the responsible independence of the associations and a comparable procedure has already been successful in the cases of the Scottish Church and of the self-governing Dominions.

If the State adopts the first method it must certainly intervene directly (and generally on behalf of the workers) in any dispute in an industry in which strikes are forbidden. If the industry is itself nationalised (as the police are) a double caution is necessary, for in such a legitimate unrest over conditions of work is easily represented as indiscipline or even sedition or treason. This is true also of the armed forces. In these two cases the position is, of course, further complicated because the nature of the service requires special conditions of obedience and discipline which would make any organised protest against unjust treatment even more suspect. The first alternative then requires either that the State itself should be the employer—and in that case that definite channels should be open for the exposure of injustice and a definite and if possible a judicial committee be constituted as a court of appeal—or that the State (since it robs the employee of his most effective weapon) should be prepared to take up his cause and if necessary to impose wages and conditions of work by law.

The General Strike. In the years before 1939 this burning topic died down; but, as it is still thought of by some partisans of the one side as a danger requiring special legislative control and by some of the other as the primary weapon of revolution, we must briefly consider it. It is to be distinguished from the cases previously considered by its object. The sympathetic strike is intended to aid a particular union to achieve its ends. If it affects the vital services the Government must intervene, but otherwise it presents no special problems. The aim of the general strike, however, is essentially revolutionary. Its object is to effect a change in the structure or policy of the Government by holding up the whole community. A sympathetic strike may be anticipated or averted by special methods of arbitration or otherwise, but a general strike cannot. It 'anticipates a condition of civil war'.[1] Revolution is no doubt sometimes justified, but this justification is the only justification for a general strike. There are two possible aims, a change of constitution or a change of government policy on some particular issue. General strikes have in the past been used for both ends. The first type may be illustrated by the strike which caused the Czar to summon the first Duma and by that which met the 'Kapp Putsch', the second by the strike which stopped the British Government from sending an anti-Russian expedition to Poland in 1920. But the procedure is revolutionary. Strikes of the second kind should rarely be defensible where there is a genuine opposition, free criticism and a democratic parliamentary system. Only when a Government has got into power and then, before its

1. J. R. Clynes at Glasgow, September 1919.

term of office endes, has developed a policy which has lost the support of the great majority of the citizens, and where immediate action is needed to save the situation and all methods of peaceful pressure and protest have failed, can there be a *prima facie* case. Here too, as always in revolution, against the value of achieving the aim must be set the cost of achieving it by so wasteful a method. It is to be noted in this last connection that only where all the above conditions are satisfied will the strike have any reasonable chance of success. For, if there is not overwhelming support for its object, the reaction of self-defence will throw the general body of citizens solidly behind the Government; and (under general strike conditions) the conduct of the Government is likely to be directed by its own most bellicose and least reasonable members, and in case of failure the results are likely to be further from the aims of the strikers than the *status quo ante*. The general strike, then, is a type of revolution demanding the same conditions for its justification as for its success. This cannot be said of any other revolutionary method, so that even the prophets of revolution are ill-advised to look to it as their weapon. But it is not a danger which legislation can anticipate or avert.

The unions and the alternative of State action. The whole position of the unions is additionally complicated by the fact that their aims are mainly economic. They are concerned with the conditions of life and not with life itself. They therefore represent nothing of ultimate spiritual significance. Their roots are in injustice and their aims are defensive. The removal of the injustice and the offence would therefore seem to abolish their *raison d'être*. The State might take over all their functions, as it has already taken some of them in paying Members of Parliament and in its health and unemployment insurance schemes. Such transfer does not destroy the spirit in the same way that State control of religion or science does. No doubt in a capitalist society unions will survive, but even so the health of that society would be largely measured by their inaction. There are, however, interests common to the workers in a particular industry, yet it is clear that most of the functions of the unions might disappear or be otherwise achieved without loss. Their actual functions therefore at any particular time will depend on historical factors and the economic methods of the State in which they are included.

The State and Churches. This section requires both apology and explanation. It may seem absurd to dismiss in a few pages a problem which has shaken the world for twenty centuries and filled whole libraries with controversy. But brevity is justified by relevance, and it is my contention throughout that the philosopher as such can say little on the detail of political problems. Such principles as he may elicit from the facts may be applied in new circumstances, but it requires practical experience and historical knowledge as well as philosophical insight to apply them.

A Church is essentially an association maintaining a doctrine, a form of worship and an ethical ideal. With the first two the State can have no claim to interfere. Not merely this, but any interference is self-defeating.[1] Here lies the contrast between the internality of a Church and the externality of a trade union. If a factory regulation is needed it does not really matter how it is achieved. If shorter hours are desirable they will do good whether they are imposed by Parliament, granted by employers, or extorted by workmen. If I am a workman I can allow other people to arrange these things for me. But I cannot get other people to do my thinking or worship for me. In this connection too it must be remembered that the Churches have been sinners as well as sufferers in the matter of freedom. The movement of a Professorship of chemistry in the University of Glasgow was halted in 1857 by religious objectors, whose spokesman, the Professor of Theology, said that a Chair of Chemistry was 'contrary to the idea of a University as it existed in the Divine Mind'. This spirit is as dangerous as any State persecution both to the Church itself (since it drives all thinking men into opposition to her) and to the development of free institutions generally (since it sets the State an example in tyranny which is all too easy to follow). The only logical attitude for a Government which denies religious liberty is that of the original Bolshevists. If religion itself is evil, then its suppression is good. But the compromises of the other dictators have always shown the inherent weakness of their claims.

The next problem is that of the internal organisation or order of the Church. I said above that it is best on the whole that an association should develop its own forms of organisation without State interference. With Churches this claim is specially strengthened, because in most cases the order and organisation is part of the doctrine which makes a Church the Church that it is. To impose a less autocratic constitution on the Miners' Federation might be unwise, but would leave its essential functions untouched. But to impose it on the Roman Catholic Church

1. See above, pp. 75–6.

would destroy Roman Catholicism itself. This is no peculiarity of Papal authority. The Archbishops and Bishops of the Church of England made the same claim in 1928. 'It is a fundamental principle that the Church—that is the Bishops, together with the clergy and laity—must in the last resort, when its mind has been fully ascertained, retain its inalienable right, in loyalty to our Lord and Saviour Jesus Christ, to formulate its faith in Him, and to arrange the expression of that Holy Faith in its forms of worship.' This claim was overridden (it is to be hoped for the last time) when Parliament rejected the Revised Prayer Book of 1928, and it is still overriden whenever political influences determine the appointment of Bishops. But the same claim made by the Church of Scotland in 1921 has been admitted by Parliament and is part of the law of the land. 'The Church, as part of the Universal Church wherein the Lord Jesus Christ has appointed a government in the hands of Church office-bearers, receives from Him, its Divine King and Head, and from Him alone, the right and power subject to no civil authority to legislate, and to adjudicate finally, in all matters of doctrine, worship, government, and discipline of the Church.'

These, then, are the positive claims of the Church for freedom which I think unassailable. The negative side requires only repetition. The State must intervene if the action of a Church leads to danger to life by riot or breach of the peace. The members and officials of the Church must be subject to criminal law; the immunity of the clergy is dead, and rightly so. As a property-owner the Church must submit to the decision of the civil courts in any matter of dispute, and keep her property in safe repair, in a sanitary condition, and so on.

There is, however, one field where a clash may come. The third characteristic of a Church noted above was the maintenance of an ethical ideal. The State in its criminal law may be said also to maintain an ethical ideal. What if these ideals diverge and contradiction follows? Any apprehension of such a clash is diminished when it is remembered that the 'maintenance' of the ideal differs greatly in the two cases. The clash would occur if a Church enjoined on its members actions which the State forbade, or forbade actions which the State enjoined. The latter case is improbable as the State's ethical orders are mainly negative. In considering the first alternative we must recall that the criminal law expresses a minimum common standard of external behaviour and must therefore lag behind the accepted level of conduct in any community.[1] The Church, on the other hand, sets a positive standard before its members, and if it is a developed and genuinely spiritual Church an impossibly high standard. The clash would therefore come only when a Church regarded as part of its 'counsels of perfection' an action so far below the general level of the community that the law forbids it. An instance of this may be found in the prosecutions of the Peculiar People, who refuse to summon doctors to their children when they fall ill because they take literally the Epistle of St James both in its silences and in its exhortations.[2] In such a case it is impossible not to ask questions about the religion involved. The clash arises because the religion is primitive. It believes (i) in the literal inspiration of the Bible, (ii) that whatever is not mentioned is prohibited, (iii) that the will of God cannot be achieved through the work of a doctor. This mixture of primitive logic and primitive theology puts the State in an impossible position. ('Suttee'—the suicide of women at the funerals of their husbands—rests on two equally primitive beliefs, that a man must take his chattels with him into the next world, and that a woman is a chattel.) The Peculiar People, however, act morally in breaking the law and must simply receive the consequences as martyrs. For in the last resort religion can always triumph and the religious man remain unsullied. The State cannot compel him to do anything against his religion but can only punish him after he has acted as his religion dictates.

These cases, however, are very exceptional. Usually, when there is said to be a clash between the two standards, this involves confused thinking. The case of divorce shows this clearly. The State recognises and provides facilities for divorce and for the remarriage of divorced persons. Some Churches forbid divorce and remarriage after it. Some recognise divorce but forbid remarriage. But the State does not *compel* anyone to be divorced, and good Catholics may continue in matrimony even in circumstances where the law would allow divorce. Nor need a good churchman marry a divorcee, though the law would allow him to do so. No Church can impose its standard on the State, but the State does not impose its standards on the Church. The Church of England is in an anomalous position here. At one time her clergy were compelled to marry divorced persons, and later they were compelled to allow the use of their churches for such marriages. This was indefensible. There exist facilities for civil marriage, and if the rules of the Church reject marriages of a certain type, no Parliament

1. See p. 99.   2. James v, 14, 15.

should have the power to impose them. If Establishment means this, better no Establishment. But the example of the Scottish Church shows that Establishment need not mean dictation. The English Church has itself been partly to blame for encouraging this error. There are already signs of a healthy revolt against the easy assumptions of last century. All recruits who have no religion are no longer deemed 'C. of E.' Nor do most Church of England chaplains regret the change which reduces their congregations from a crowd of conscripts to the handful of believers which their Roman Catholic or Presbyterian colleagues have always had. Again, the use of the Church for baptism, marriage and burial by people who never otherwise set foot inside it, or show any other sign of Christian belief or practice, is now becoming recognised as a source not of strength but of weakness to the Church. But as long as she welcomes 'no-religion' soldiers to her church parades and 'no-religion' couples to her Marriage Service she must not be surprised at a demand for 'no-religion' divorce and remarriage by her ministers or within her buildings.

The conflict of Church and State over ethical standards is therefore one so unusual as to offer no serious difficulty. But the action of the State is not limited to criminal law, and other fields do reveal conflict. The most notorious of these cases concerns the attitude of the State to war and to her own continued existence. When Pilate was faced with his problem, he saw no clash of moral standards; he thought he saw a threat to Roman sovereignty. The general problem of war is a difficult one, but here I need assume only one point, namely that fighting in self-defence is justifiable. There are of course many high-principled men who reject this view. In the War of 1914–1918 England exempted such objectors in principle, though the composition of local tribunals and the hysteria of public opinion made the application of the law difficult and sometimes impossible. In the War of 1939–1945 hysteria was less marked and the application of the law was fair and reasonable. These exemptions are possible because genuine pacifists are few and many of them are prepared to do non-combatant duties. Let us imagine, however, a country attacked by a barbaric and 'totalitarian' enemy and containing a minority of Quakers so large that their exemption would ensure military defeat for their country. It would seem in that case that the government should introduce conscription without exemptions. This would force those of weaker faith to fight. The government would have to punish those whose faith held out, though it would admire

E

them the more. Its justification would be that conquest by the invader would be the end not merely of national independence, but (far more certainly) of Quakerism also. I agree that the position into which such a government is driven is an 'impossible' one, that is to say a position in which no solution avoids absolute wrong. But this only confirms the conclusion that war as such is wrong. So also in everyday life I may be 'put in an impossible position' by someone else's wrong-doing, and in that case the 'someone else' is to blame. It is one of the strongest arguments against war that it leads to such insoluble dilemmas—to the punishment of men because of their devotion, to the necessity of sending men to their death, because they are better men than their fellows, to the suppression of what is intrinsically good in the hope that finally a greater good may be achieved.

The Church can then claim absolute freedom for her doctrines, her forms of worship, and the inculcation of her moral standards. She must render absolute obedience in the fields where the State is supreme—peace, security, order, health and contract.

One final difficulty emerges. The Church claims to cover the whole of life. Should she not engage in politics in the attempt to further those ends which are part of her moral ideal—social justice and peace? 'Christian Socialism' and the support by Churches in their corporate capacity of the League of Nations or of Prohibition raised this question. I think such political action inadvisable. Its dangers have been seen in many continental countries where 'clerical' parties have degraded the life of the Church and produced wholly intelligible reactions. In the Spanish Civil War the 'sacrilege' of the Spanish militiamen had been rendered inevitable by the previous political activities of the clergy. Individuals must certainly help to remove injustice, and a Christian's voice and vote will be likely to back reform or peace. But official corporate action is a different matter. When a priest treats his own servants justly or a Christian reconciles two enemies we do not speak of 'Church interference in private matters', and Church intervention in politics should be exactly of this type and nothing more.

13

THE STATE AND OTHER STATES

The first problem raised by the relations between States is that of
international morality. Discussions in preceding chapters have
cleared up some of the issues here. The view that relations between States are non-moral is a corollary of the view we have
rejected, that the State is the ultimate moral authority, and need
not further concern us here. The problem remains whether the
principles of international morality are identical with those of
individual morality, or whether there are moral principles with
special application to international relations only. In dealing with
this issue, some points argued elsewhere may be restated. Firstly,
moral rules derive from moral values. These values are the same
for national and international decisions. But since the rules are
directed to achieve the values they may vary with circumstances
and may therefore differ in the two fields. Secondly, 'the good of
a State' or 'the national interest' must be analysable into the
interests of individual citizens; anything claimed to be a 'national
interest' and not so analysable is an illusion and a false goal of
policy. Thirdly, a State is not a moral agent. International morality therefore means either the morality of citizens of one State in
their relations with citizens of other States or the morality of
the government of one State in relation to governments and
citizens of other States.[1]

As between citizens of different States, in their direct relations
with each other, there are no moral principles differing from those
holding between citizens of the same State, save that member-

1. See next chapter.

ship of the same State (like common membership of any other association) gives priority to the claims of fellow-members. I have duties to save the life of a foreigner, to pay my debts to him, to spare him unnecessary suffering, to help save him from disease or starvation, so far as I can, and so on. But citizens of my own State have always a special claim on my assistance.

The real problem concerns the duties of governments. A government may be tempted to take the view that in foreign affairs it should consider only the interests of its own country on the ground that it is a position of trust. (The same argument is often used by representatives of other bodies; a trade union leader, for example, may regard himself as bound to uphold solely the interests of its own members whenever there is a conflict of interests.) This view, however, would mean that international relations would be reduced to 'power politics' and subject to no moral considerations, a conclusion we have already rejected as untenable. A milder variant of this extreme view would be that a government need not be precluded from acting in the interests of another country, provided its own interests are not affected; but, in any conflict, it must put the interests of its own people first. Even this view, however, is fundamentally non-moral. It would mean that no government could commit its own people to a small sacrifice for the very much greater good of another people. (All these problems have had striking illustrations recently in the question of allocation of food supplies.) Yet the argument that the government is in a position of trust retains considerable force despite these admissions. For it is clearly impossible to treat a government as if it were an individual, whose moral duty is often measured by the degrees of sacrifice he makes of his own interests to others. The truth surely is that a government is in a position comparable with that of any individual who has accepted a commitment (e.g. made a promise). There are occasions when, to achieve a great and obvious good or avert a great and obvious evil, a promise should be broken. There are occasions when similarly a government may subject the interests of its own citizens to those of others. The degree of good achieved or evil averted which is required to tip the scale must depend on the circumstances (as it does in the promise case) and cannot be generally laid down.

A special complicating factor—and one which permeates all international relations—is the attitude of other governments. If they follow their own national interests alone, our Government will be compelled to put our national interest first in every conflict. (It will not be compelled to follow our national interest *alone*, because it would still be able to pursue the interest of another people when it did not conflict with our own.) Similarly a trade union leader, in negotiation with employers who show no regard whatever for the interests of their workers, must take a tough line and give away nothing except what cannot damage his own members' interests.

A special problem of international morality concerns the continuity of international obligations. Are successive governments bound by commitments incurred by their predecessors in office? Normally the obligation stands, though it is subject to the general consideration that changed circumstances may annul it. A guarantee of the frontiers of a State does not bind the guarantors to uphold frontiers extended by subsequent aggression. A particular exception may be held to arise in the case of a revolutionary change of government (as in the repudiation by the Soviet Government of the debts of Czarist Russia). Where such debts were incurred by the pre-revolutionary government in order to acquire arms to suppress revolution, the repudiation is reasonable. For the lenders would have had their eyes open to the risk. Where, on the other hand, the loan to the pre-revolutionary government was for essential public services—food supply, for example—or for constructive work whose benefits accrue to the citizens of the borrowing country regardless of the revolution—housing or railway construction, for example—the repudiation is unjustifiable; for it would mean that these benefits were being provided at the expense of foreigners. A further case where repudiation can be defended may arise when an opposition party announces its intention to repudiate debts incurred by the government in office if it comes to power. Those who lend to the government after such an announcement take a risk with their eyes open. (The position is parallel to that of a husband who publishes his intention not to be responsible for his wife's debts.) Apart from these relatively clear cases it is not possible to lay down any rule, though in general the onus is obviously on the defaulting government to find special and overriding justification for repudiation. The same arguments apply throughout to other commitments. Commitments undertaken in pursuit of a foreign policy steadily and publicly attacked and disowned by a party in opposition are not fully binding on that party when it comes into office, though their repudiation must take account of interests, e.g. of third

parties, which would be adversely affected by complete repudiation.

The fact that these complex and, in some respects, indeterminate conclusions are necessary is in itself a support of the general
position maintained in this book, namely that it is impossible to
treat States as moral persons. For such treatment would involve
either that States were above morality and in a Hobbistic state
of war with each other in which self-interest was the guiding
principle; or else that they were bound by the same moral
principles as individuals are. Neither conclusion is defensible,
and any solution must take account of the relations between
governments and their own peoples, including opposition
parties.

The second main problem of international relations is that of
international organisation. It was noted above[1] that, for many of
the purposes achieved by the State, the State is itself too small a
unit. Security of life is menaced from abroad as well as from at
home. Crime crosses frontiers, as do disputes of the types dealt
with by civil law. Public health is menaced by epidemics in other
countries. Economic welfare and standards of life involve the
whole world.

It would seem from all these considerations and many others
like them that the State has outlived its usefulness.

Until recently all these problems were dealt with on a basis
of complete national sovereignty by each State taking its own
precautions or supplementing these by international agreements.
A State met the menace to security from beyond its own frontiers
by fortifications and armies; it added, if it felt its security required them, alliances and mutual guarantees with other States.
International crime was met by extradition treaties, the threat
of disease by quarantine, and again, if necessary, by international
agreement. Economic security and standards of living were
defended by tariffs and trade agreements. In all this area there was
little or no international organisation and little or no international
law.

Where there was such organisation, as in the Hague Court or
the Postal Union, it bound only such governments as freely under-
took to employ it. As a result all international obligations had
to be unanimously accepted by those States who were bound by
them.

The first step beyond this state of affairs is normally the erec-

1. See pp. 98–100.

tion of international advisory bodies which can recommend action which it is still open to any State to refuse to implement. The work of the League of Nations was largely of this character (e.g. in protection of minorities or in the application of sanctions against an aggressor). Such methods, backed by full publicity, have considerable weight.

A further step is taken when States bind themselves in general terms to carry out any decisions taken by the international body to which they adhere, and where their consent is not required for every particular decision. This is the stage reached by the Charter of the United Nations and in particular by the provisions concerning the powers of the Security Council. It is presumably still possible for a State to avoid the fulfilment of its obligations under the Charter (for example, its obligations to submit disputes to the United Nations Organisation or to assist the Security Council to repress aggression, by withdrawing from the Organisation altogether. For this reason, and because the initial obligation is freely accepted by the signing of the Charter, the complete sovereignty of State Members is still retained in theory. But it is clear that, if the Organisation is successful, complete freedom of action, at least in regard to international peace and security, will have disappeared. And there is at least one article in the Charter which explicitly removes even this general form of consent. 'The Organisation shall ensure that States which are not members of the United Nations act in accordance with these Principles so far as may be necessary for the maintenance of international peace and security.'[1] Thus a State may escape its obligations, but would not escape the further attentions of the Organisation by resigning from it.

There are good reasons for believing that the authority of an international organisation cannot for the present advance beyond the limits now reached.

The first is the actual power of national feeling. Ultimate authority has been so firmly consolidated in the Nation-State that it would seem to require a solvent having the force of a religion to break down the barriers which national loyalties have erected. No reasons of administrative efficiency or practical convenience would seem sufficient for this purpose. Christianity in principle ought to be such a force; and international communism might well be an alternative. But Christianity has now settled down into a religious belief detached from secular authority and

1. *Charter of the United Nations*, ch. I, Art 2., cl. 6.

no longer claiming to be a source of law. And communism; for the present at any rate, is handicapped for the task of overriding State barriers by being firmly attached to the interests of a single State.

There are further reasons why the erection of a World-State at present would appear impossible. It has been shown above that criminal law is one of the spheres of State action, and that criminal law must reflect the general moral standards of the inhabitants of the State on which it is imposed. But these standards vary, as also do the attitudes of peoples towards law itself, from country to country. So that anything like a universal criminal code is out of the question. It might be thought that criminal law could remain a matter of local jurisdiction, while civil law, economic affairs, health regulations, etc., became subject to international control. But the interactions and overlapping between these fields and criminal law are so great and so widespread that such a division of authority would appear unworkable. Civil suits give rise to criminal proceedings—for perjury or false pretences for example. Economic organisation can hardly be kept clear from questions of social justice, private property, etc., which are fundamentally moral issues on which peoples differ and demand different solutions. Public health raises such questions as prohibition, prostitution, birth-control, where again moral standards are involved.

Another drawback to the concentration of authority in an international organisation is that concentration would further increase the difficulties, already sufficiently serious, of maintaining touch between governments and their peoples. In a genuinely democratic country free criticism is able to make itself felt by the government; elections and the existence of opposition parties ensure the possibility of peaceful change of policy; debates and broadcasting enable the government to explain its policy so that those who follow it can follow intelligently and not blindly. The leaders of the government can be known to their people and can even establish with them some sort of personal contact. All these processes, already threatened by the centralisation and complexity of the Nation-State, would be rendered impracticable in a World-State: such a World-State would be inevitably bureaucratic in its methods and authoritarian in its attitude.

The same tendency would seem to be inevitable if looked at from another angle. If there were to arise a movement which should have the quasi-religious authority necessary to override national loyalties in the hearts of men, it would have to be a movement making at least as sweeping claims on men's lives as nationalism does.

We shall see later, however, that the claim of the State to monopolise loyalty, devotion and service is a dangerous and inacceptable claim. We shall see also that the attempt to back this claim by harnessing nationalism or any other ideology to the State's service is fraught with further dangers.[1] Thus the prospect of superseding national loyalty by a world loyalty resting on something comparable to national feeling is not wholly desirable. A totalitarian State, even if it embraced the whole world, would still be evil because totalitarian.

If, for all these reasons, the problems of international relations should not be solved along the direction of wider political units, is there no alternative direction? In previous chapters of this book we looked for the solution of the problem of political authority by means of a definition of the spheres in which State action was essential. We treated State action as only one alternative method of producing good or countering evil—and one which (because of its denial of liberty) requires special justification on each occasion, in contrast with private effort or voluntary association. The same line of thought can be followed here.

The hope for the future is not that national interests and political loyalties should be expanded to cover wider units, but that the emphasis should be taken off national and political divisions altogether. If frontiers could come to be regarded only as the limits of administrative areas, with movements of men, goods and ideas flowing freely across them, there would be a chance for an international co-operation which would not rest on a primarily political basis. It is noticeable already that the non-political organs of international organisation work more smoothly than the political organs. The International Labour Organisation, the Postal Union, the Opium Control Committee, the Food and Agriculture Organisation—these are the real hopes of the future. While the Security Council is likely for many generations to be a focus of suspicion, hostility, mistrust and fear, just because it necessarily presupposes a world of national power-politics, these other bodies should have a better chance of positive and creative work. The work of the Security Council—even if it were completely successful—would remain negative; the avoidance of war, the suppression of aggression, the control of armaments, etc. The

1. See ch. 15.

positive contribution to human welfare must come from co-operation on technical problems.

A special difficulty about such technical co-operation is that it also must be conducted on a basis of government representation. For, if the international organ reaches decisions requiring general regulation, such regulations can be imposed only by governments. Thus an international health organisation attended by non-governmental health experts only would remain a research and advisory body.

There are two solutions to this difficulty. One is to keep running, alongside the official organisation, the maximum amount of technical intercommunication between workers in similar fields, on either side of every frontier. The other is for governments to select their representatives on such official organisations from the laboratory, the field and the workshop as well as from the Ministry concerned. Both these methods have already taken root in this country.

No doubt such a picture of complex and various 'functional organisations' for health, food, drugs, exchange, etc., is Utopian. But it is less Utopian and fundamentally less dangerous than the picture of a world unified by an international spirit replacing the old nationalisms and drawing to itself the loyalties they now attract. It is also a picture which can be filled in gradually and piece by piece by a process which draws on the natural tendency of experts to understand each other and of men working for a limited, clear and positive objective to be able to achieve results which statesmen and politicians would find impossible.

(D)
The unity of the State

14

THE GENERAL WILL AND THE
CORPORATE SELF

In dealing with Rousseau and the idealist philosophy of politics which descended from him we left over a part of his theory which to many of his followers supplies its real force. We considered the view that morality is exhausted in State service and obedience to the State's commands. This view of morality is supported in Rousseau and his followers by a psychology which renders subservient to the State all individual choice and action.

The comparison of State and individual is as old as Plato; but until Rousseau the comparison stopped short at an insistence on the organic nature of the State. It held that citizens must all contribute to the common good; that if one suffers the whole body must suffer; that a man cut off from his State is enfeebled and mutilated. In Rousseau, however, the State is said to be a 'self' in a much wider sense. 'The act of association creates a moral and collective body composed of as many members as the assembly contains votes, and receiving from this act its unity, its common life and its will.'[1] 'The body politic is a moral being possessed of a will.'[2] Thus the State can be said to have purposes and set out to achieve them, to be intelligent and responsible. Before considering this conception of corporate personality we may note briefly the use to which it is put.

The will of the State is identified with the wills of the citizens. When it is observed that State and citizen may conflict, it is then said that the will of the State is the better or higher self of the

1. *Contrat Social*, I, vi.
2. *Discourse on Political Economy* (Everyman Edition, 1946, p. 236).

citizen, his moral, permanent, rational or real will. There is an exact parallel between this view and the conception of Divine Immanence in the human soul. As it is the latter conception alone which can regard the service of God as 'perfect freedom', so also in political theory this view makes it possible to regard the State's claims or orders as the voice of my higher self and not as the tyranny of an external force. As in the progress from Old Testament to New Testament theology the concept of an external Judge gives way to that of an indwelling Spirit, so here the idea of an imposed law and sovereignty yields to the idea of a self-imposed moral standard, to self-expression and self-control. By this bold stroke liberty and political obligation are identified, and even a criminal may be 'forced to be free'.[1] On this view, also, it is impossible to admit that State action is immoral. The State can do no wrong. Nor, strictly speaking, can State action be moral. For morality means the triumph in me of the corporate self over the private self; and in the State itself this division is meaningless. So while Rousseau held that the General Will is always morally right, Hegel was more accurate in maintaining that the State was above morality and immorality equally.

With this application of the idea of State personality I shall not deal directly. For, if the whole notion of State personality is found to be indefensible, its applications will fall without further discussion.

There is another direction in which the notion of corporate personality has developed which will make easier our discussion of it and which has itself been used as an attack on Rousseau and Hegel. If the act of association creates a corporate self, then there must be many such selves other than States. The study of thèse 'selves' has recently become a special branch of psychology. Le Bon has studied the crowd, Trotter the herd, and McDougall armies and nations. With the detail of their observations the philosopher is not concerned. But he is concerned with the concepts they use to interpret these observations. I have dealt in a previous section with the fallacies by which such fictitious entities as 'Society' or 'the Community' are fabricated.[2] It will now advance our enquiry if I apply the same type of argument to 'the crowd'. McDougall says: 'We may sum up the psychological characters of the unorganised or simple crowd by saying that it is excessively emotional, violent, fickle, inconsistent, irresolute and

1. Rousseau, *Contrat Social*, I, vii.   2. See pp. 77–84.

extreme in action, displaying only the coarser emotions and less
refined sentiments; extremely suggestible, careless in deliberation,
hasty in judgment, incapable of any but the simpler and imperfect
forms of reasoning; easily swayed and led, lacking in self-
consciousness, devoid of self-respect and sense of responsibility,
apt to be carried away by the consciousness of its own force, so
that it tends to produce all the manifestations we have learned
to expect of any irresponsible and absolute power. Hence its
behaviour is like that of an unruly child or an untutored passion-
ate savage in a strange situation, rather than like that of its aver-
age member.'[1] Now McDougall expressly defends the view that
this language is literally accurate—that a crowd has *a mind* which
has the above characteristics. What I wish to maintain is that
there is no such entity as a crowd mind. There are only the minds
of individuals. Crowd psychology should be the study of the behaviour of men in crowds and not the behaviour of crowds.
Everywhere throughout McDougall's chapter the words 'men in
crowds' could be written in place of 'crowds' or 'the crowd' without any loss whatever. Whether these statements are true (when
written in either form) is a matter for empirical observation.
(Mr S. B. Ward, in an interesting article,[2] has some very pertinent
doubts and objections on this subject.) But the present question
is whether, even if they are true, they require the concept of a
corporate or collective mind for their interpretation. (This process of analysis does not imply a return to 'abstract individual
psychology' or assume that the individual mind can be studied in
isolation from the groups to which individuals belong. If the
crowd-psychologists are right in their empirical observations, it
makes a difference to a man's psychological reactions when he
becomes part of a crowd. But the same is true of ordinary hypnosis
as regards a man's relations to the hypnotist. Yet we do not
require a new unit [hypnotist + victim] to explain these pheno-
mena. Similarly, analysis cannot be said to treat a crowd as a
'mere aggregate', or sum of individuals, if it admits [and if the
facts justify the admission] that local togetherness and some identity of interest create new psychological tendencies in the individual
mind.) Why does it matter which form of words we use? Apart
from the question of fact—whether these are collective minds or
not—there are other serious questions of implication. If there is
a crowd mind other than the minds of the members, that mind is

1. *The Group Mind*, p. 45.
2. *Mind*, N.S. vol. XXXIII (1924), p. 275.

responsible for what the crowd does *and the members are not*. It would be proper to punish a crowd for its sins *but improper to punish any member*. These are impossible contradictions. Yet men fall into them. They do suffer from (and indeed often welcome) this illusion of shelved responsibility.

Since a crowd is an unorganised group there is no reason to regard it as a social unit for any other purpose, once its claims to psychological unity have been dismissed. Crowds and mobs, therefore, should follow 'Society' and 'Community' off the stage of social and political theory. Their appearance, like that of the ghost of Banquo, only creates confusion.

It would seem likely at first sight that organised associations would be in a completely different position. But we now have to face the possibility that the same type of analysis which has disposed of the 'crowd mind' may be turned against all associations with equal effect. The suggestion would be that sentences in which 'Germany' or 'the Miners' Federation' or 'the British Army' occur are 'systematically misleading'.[1] They suggest that there are entities with these names which have characteristics and perform actions when in fact the characteristics and the actions are really those of individuals. The work of 'analysis' consists not of analysing a non-existent entity but of rewriting the sentences so that the misleading subject is replaced by real subjects. In the case of the crowd the rewriting was easy, since it involved only a simple substitution of the words 'men in a crowd' for the words 'the crowd'. In some cases, however, the rewriting involves a more thorough transformation. Two examples from other fields, where analysis is obviously necessary and successful, will serve to illustrate this more thorough transformation. 'Fashion is taking six inches off skirts this spring.' Now everyone knows that there is no such entity as 'fashion'. Moreover, it will not do to substitute for 'fashion' some other subject and leave the rest of the sentence standing. For again everyone knows that no skirts are actually being truncated. The analysis would have to be some such sentence as the following: 'Skirts on sale in the more expensive shops this spring will be six inches shorter than skirts on sale last autumn.' Similarly, 'Public opinion has veered round in support of the Prime Minister' must be rewritten 'There are more people who now believe in the Prime Minister's policy than there were previously'.

1. Cf. *Systematically Misleading Expressions*, Professor G. Ryle (Proceedings of the Aristotelian Society, 1931–32).

Now can this kind of analysis be applied to all associations? In the first place it must be admitted that simple substitution-analysis is often possible. In sentences such as 'England is free from bubonic plague', 'Yugoslavia is starving', sentences with 'all' or 'most' Englishmen or Yugoslavs as their subjects, are directly obtainable. But in 'Britain has sent an ultimatum to Germany' the real senders are the British Government; and the ordinary citizens may be unaware of the deed (as they certainly are in the case of 'Britain was engaged in secret negotiations with France'). I think it must be agreed that all statements attributing psychological or moral characteristics to associations require analysis. And, as a first approximation, it may be said that, in any such statement about a State, verbs of 'doing' have the government as their real subject, verbs of 'suffering' have the people as their real subject. All too often the failure to apply this analysis is one of the buttresses of tyranny. 'If a country wants war, it must suffer for it.' This sentence would seem to indicate the country's foresight and willing sacrifice. But too often the analysis should be 'If the government of a country wants war, the people must suffer for it'. The fact that actions of a State are normally the actions of its government does not, of course, mean that the full moral responsibility for these actions must lie with the government. At the one extreme there are actions carried out by a democratic government in the execution of a programme which was their main 'plank' at the election which returned them to power, or in the application of a law which has been subjected to and passed by a referendum. For these actions the majority of the people bear a large share of responsibility. They do not bear the whole responsibility because the programme is the government's programme as well as the people's choice, and the decisions on the way in which it was presented to the people, the degree to which it is applied, and the methods used to apply it are all governmental responsibilities. At the other extreme there are actions carried out by a totalitarian government in a one-party State where opposition is banned and critics are liquidated. If in addition the actions are unknown to the mass of the people, the responsibility is almost wholly that of the government. Not wholly, however, since even totalitarian one-party governments do not achieve power or retain it without considerable popular support. Intermediate between these extremes come probably all State actions and the degrees of responsibility of the government and of the people will vary as the case approaches one extreme

F

or the other. One particular point is to be noted. The fact that the people bear some responsibility for a government action does not necessarily diminish there sponsibility of the government. If the German people knew about the concentration camps their responsibility is greater than if they did not. But it does not follow that the responsibility of Himmler was lessened thereby: The only case in which the responsibility of the government might clearly be said to be lessened is in the case of an action forced on a government against its better judgment by referendum or public opinion. (The failure to rearm this country in 1933–1938 or the dropping of the Hoare-Laval plan might be quoted as examples of such a situation.) Even then the government in a democratic country would have the duty of making clear to the people just what the issues were, and might even have the duty of resigning if the people persisted in a policy which the government could not conscientiously accept.

The practical importance of such painful analysis became obvious after the last war. 'The German people were guilty and the Nazis were their tools.' 'The Nazis were guilty and the German people were their dupes.' Somewhere between these extremes the truth must have lain. 'The guilt of Germany' was subjected to such practically applied analysis at Nuremberg, and indeed everywhere in Germany where allied Control Commission officers 'screened' applicants for posts.

If it is granted that statements attributing psychological or moral characteristics to organised associations require analysis, the question remains whether there are any statements about such associations which are not so analysable. If these bodies are not units from the point of view of ethics or psychology, are they to be considered to be units for any other purpose?

There might seem to be three types of statement applicable to associations without further analysis: (i) statements about organisation; (ii) statements about legal or economic characteristics; (iii) statements in which the association is not the subject but the object of a psychological or moral attitude such as love or loyalty.

Organisation. When I say a State is happy, I mean that its citizens are happy; when I say a State is treacherous, I mean that its government is treacherous. But when I say a State is feudal or democratic or highly organised or well disciplined I do not mean that any particular persons have any of these characteristics. Here, however, analysis obviously reveals not *characteristics* of indivi-

duals but *relations* between them. For this reason it is again wrong
to say that analysis treats a State or any other association as a
mere aggregate.[1] To say a State is feudal is to assert that there are
certain relations between the individuals in it in virtue of their
rank or status. There may, however, be a doubt whether relational
statements completely eliminate a corporate unit. For example,
it may be said that a human body is a unit as real as a cell and
that cells behave as they do and are related as they are because
they form part of a human body. The relations here may be held
to be derivative and not ultimate. If, however, we apply this to
organisational characteristics of an association, the parallel breaks
down. Does the democratic character of a State account for the
facts that its government is elected and keeps in touch with its
people? Or is the statement that a State is democratic merely
another way of stating these facts? Is it because an army is well
disciplined that lower ranks obey orders unquestionably? Or
when we call an army well disciplined are we simply restating these
relationships between higher and lower ranks? In each case the
latter alternative is clearly the correct one. There is no further
quality of democracy or discipline from which these relationships
are derived. Though a group of men united by such relationships
is no mere aggregate, it is still not a new unit with curious characters of its own.

Economic and legal characteristics. These cases again are more
difficult, and it is probably here that the belief in corporate personality has its strongest roots. One of our greatest lawyers has said:
'When a body of 20 or 2000 or 20,000 men bind themselves
together to act in a particular way for a common purpose, they
create a body which by no fiction of the law but by the very nature
of things differs from the individuals of which it was constituted.'[2]
Analysis here seems to fail. 'Liverpool is a moral city' means that
Liverpudlians are moral men. 'But 'Liverpool is rich' does not
necessarily mean that Liverpudlians are wealthy men (though this
is one possible meaning of it). The words 'is rich' may mean just
what they do in 'Jones is rich', and Liverpool may be the true
subject. Other economic attributes which appear really to belong to
associations and not at the same time to their members are:
solvent, bankrupt, lavish, spendthrift.

The same is true of legal concepts. An association may be an
employer, an employee, a contracting party or a defaulting debtor;
in just the same way as an individual is. (The work of Gierke and

1. Cf. above, pp.143–4.   2. Dicey.

Maitland has done much to establish this legal point.) In the same
way, in trade, a man may be quite unaware whether he is dealing
with a company or with an individual, and normally it makes no
difference at all which it is.

Now these cases must be admitted as they stand. Where the
above simple-seeming economic or legal concepts are taken as
ultimate, then they may belong to associations in exactly the
same sense as they belong to individuals, and their attribution to
associations is not analysable into their attribution to individuals.
If 'rich' means holding large capital assets in cash or securities,
an association may be rich while its members are poor. If 'solvent'
means having a balance of income over expenditure, and if
'prosperous' indicates that this balance is increasing, then an
association may be solvent or prosperous while its members are
bankrupt or go downhill. If we stop short with 'money values',
we must treat men and associations as equally units for economics,
neither more ultimate than the other. Behind money, however,
stands the whole field of human needs and desires; and economics
must become ultimately a branch of mathematics, or lead back
into morals and psychology and again to an analysis in terms of
individuals. Wealth, prosperity, value—these take us in the end
beyond money economics and they take us to men as our units.

So also with legal concepts. A legal concept may have a purely
legal mark or aspect; and in this respect associations may count
as legal individuals. But this legal aspect is, even for the lawyer,
insufficient to exhaust the concept; and other aspects require
analysis in terms of individuals. 'Ownership', for example, may
mean simply the occurrence of a name on a title deed; and in this
respect a field or mountain may be 'owned' by George Glasgow,
by Glasgow & Co., or by the Corporation of Glasgow. But ownership also means a complex of powers of behaviour. When I own
something I can do certain things with it. But these powers of
behaviour can belong only to individuals. When a city owns a
field or a mountain, this may mean that its inhabitants may play
in the field or walk on the mountain, or that its officers may work
the minerals or its employees cut the timber there. But the city
cannot walk or dig or cut down trees. Trustee Law and Company
Law set out what in fact are the powers and obligations of the
various persons concerned, so far as the Trust Deeds or Articles
of Association do not define these. It used to be held that a Corporation was legally *persona ficta*—a fictitious person. Perhaps it
would be more accurate to say that all legal persons, including

individuals, are *personae fictae* in the sense that their powers are legally defined.

The association as a psychological objective. I am here using 'objective' in Meinong's sense, as the correlate of a psychological state which has a transitive character. For instance, 'England loved Victoria' shows Victoria as a psychological objective. And here 'England' is simply analysable into 'all' or 'most' Englishmen. But 'Victoria loved England' has 'England' as its objective, and a similar analysis of 'England' appears impossible. Another way of raising the same issue is to ask what loyalty and patriotism are. It is possible of course for loyalty, in a general sense, to be felt to any cause—to principles or to persons. In particular, loyalty to a country may mean loyalty to the ideals for which the country stands or loyalty to fellow-citizens as such. The latter is a particular example of the claims of fellow-members of any association, a claim we have already admitted. The former loyalty if, it is what it claims to be, requires no defence. Loyalty to ideals is unexceptionable. But in that case the loyalty should cease if the country deserted its ideals and should be felt equally to any other association which supported them. This is seldom the case. The loyal citizen of France believes that France stands for certain values, but supports those values in part at least because they are held in honour by France. Similarly with love. Love of country may be explained as the love of certain scents and sounds, of land-scapes or buildings.[1] But these scents and sounds might be created in a laboratory without yielding the same result; and similar landscapes in Sweden or buildings in New Hampshire might equally fail. These things are all loved in part at least because they are English. Over them is woven a web of familiarity and ease, of tradition and history. The form of the question 'Why do you love your country?' suggests indeed that any answer must fail. Even if the answer comes that I love her for her hills and valleys, her traditions of liberty and tolerance, her ideals and achieve-ments, I still seem to be asserting that she is more than all these things. To some indeed the question itself would seem a blas-phemy. Love of country should be a virtue as ultimate as courage or temperance and should require as little defence. The analysis of loyalty or patriotism thus appears to be either impertinent or impossible. In the extreme case these feelings are dissociated altogether from the ideals for which the country stands and the service of the citizens of whom it is composed. 'My country right

1. See pp. 50, 51.

or wrong' typifies the first of these dissociations; the second is
illustrated by the slogan with which good Nazis were exhorted
to greet every sunrise: '*Du bist Nichts; dein Volk ist Alles*'—'You
are nothing; your people is everything'. The first slogan is obviously indefensible. The second is characteristic of the illusions
created by the notion of corporate personality; if all individual
Nazis are nothing, the Nazi people is nothing too.

The truth is that the theory of 'psychological objectives' from
which we set out is itself at fault. Fear and love and hate are
feelings which ought to have objects, but sometimes have none.
'Jones fears ghosts' means that Jones believes that certain noises,
etc., are caused by disembodied yet localised spirits, and Jones is
afraid. The fear would be reasonable if the belief were true and
the objects existed. Stesichorus held that the Greeks at Troy
fought for a phantom Helen; and the patriotism which counts
the individual as nothing and the *Volk* or the State or the Nation
as everything is fighting for shadows too. A lover's illusions
about the perfections of his mistress may centre around a real
woman, however much she differs from the woman of his dreams.
A patriot's illusions concerning national greatness and national
honour, about his country's prestige and pride, also centre around
realities—the honour of his government and the welfare of its
individual subjects. But his illusion creates no further object other
than land and men, and land is no object of devotion. 'For men
make up the city, and not walls nor ships empty of men.'[1] The
two most potent factors inducing such beliefs (apart from the
artificial aids of education and propaganda) are the human desires
for service and survival. There is little one man can do to change
the face of the world; but if he identifies himself with the
greatness and glory of his country (or indeed of any association)
he can work with pride and confidence. The men who drove the
rivets into the Forth Bridge were said to have felt this pride of
creation in the whole great work. This is no mean ideal, but it is
childish picture-thinking which mistakes symbol for fact and
substitutes for the difficult notion of a complex of persons co-
operating in the service of an ideal or of other persons the easier
idea of service of a single unit. Perhaps more subtle still is the
desire for immortality. I do so little and with my life all is ended.
Here again picture-thinking substitutes for the difficult ideas of
true eternity and true immortality the easier notion of continuance in the world of space and time. The Chinese feel themselves

1. Thucydides.

immortal in their families. But mere continuance of a family cannot overleap the grave, as the Chinese admit when they recognise that to leave behind bad or ungrateful children does not confer an equal immortality. So too with the State. 'Who dies if England live?' This question which seems to take victory from the grave can do so only if no other questions are asked. Is 'England' a name for an aggressive and expanding domination?

> Wider still and wider shall thy bounds be set;
> God who made thee mighty make thee mightier yet!

Few can now feel wholly satisfied by this. Yet the dissatisfaction can only be resolved by asking 'analytic' questions. If this is what we are asked to die for, who is the better for it? If the cynics are right and we are really being asked to die for markets for our industries or raw materials for our manufacturers or for land from which natives must be excluded so that our retired officers may settle there, let us know it, even if, knowing it, we shall feel less ready to die for these aims than if they are called 'the greatness and glory of England'. Or is 'England' a name for certain ideals of life and government?

> The England of my dreams is she,
> Long hoped and long deferred,
> Who always promises to be
> And always breaks her word.[1]

If so, then it is not England but her ideals themselves which should inspire us. We may then attack some of the ideals for which England stands[2] and we should be able to do this without hearing the cry of 'traitor'. Yet we shall hear it, and from those whom mythology and illusion have led captive, and who believe in the ideals because they are English, and not vice versa as they should.

Yet this demand for continuance will die hard. Sorrow over impermanence is a legacy of the Romantic Movement fortified by Pauline theology. We have to relearn that the Kingdom of Heaven is within us, and that the value of anything is not affected by what is left of it after a thousand years. The lesson ought not to be too hard, for every man knows that the things he thinks most worth doing are not required to produce deferred interest.

1. William Watson.
2. Cf. *This England* (the *New Statesman* anthology).

Ask the musician or the mountaineer what survives from his playing or climbing. You may puzzle him and he may think up answers, but they will be false answers or at any rate not his real answers. (William Byrd's 'Reasons' may have been useful 'to perswade every one to learne to sing', but not one of them was his reason for singing. They were:

1. It is a knowledge easely taught. . . .
2. The exercise of singing is delightful to Nature and good to preserve the health of Man.
3. It doth strengthen all parts of the brest, and doth open the pipes.
4. It is a singular good remedie for a stutting and stamaring in the speech.
5. It is the best means to procure a perfect pronunciation. . . .
6. It is the only way to know where Nature hath bestowed the benefit of a good voyce. . . .
7. There is not any Musicke of Instruments whatsoever comparable to that which is made of the voyces of men. . . .
8. The better the voyce is, the meeter it is to honour and serve God there-with. . . .)[1]

We must escape this domination of time. 'Our world and every other possible world are from one side worthless equally. . . . The differences of past and future, of dream and waking, of "on earth" or elsewhere, are one and all immaterial. Our life has value only because and so far as it realises in fact that which transcends time and existence. Goodness, beauty, and truth are all there is which in the end is real. . . . "For love and beauty and delight", it is no matter where they have shown themselves, "there is no death nor change" and this conclusion is true. These things do not die since the Paradise in which they bloom is immortal. That Paradise is no special region nor any given particular spot in time and space. It is here, it is everywhere where any finite being is lifted into that higher life which alone is waking reality.'[2] And what Bradley said of the Kingdom of Heaven is true of the United Kingdom also. We must press our questions unremittingly. We must ask 'Why are we in Gibraltar or the Solomon Islands?' We must ask our politicians, 'Why are we nationalising this or resisting the nationalisation of that?' We must ask ourselves whether indeed all that is British is best. Against these searching

1. Preface to *Psalms, Sonets, and Songs of sadness and pietie* (1588).
2. F. H. Bradley, *Essays on Truth and Reality*, pp. 468, 469.

questions we shall find two centuries of popular theology, twenty centuries of racial suspicion and fear, two hundred centuries of the domination of emotion and imagination over reason and truth. But on our side we can enlist satire and humour, honesty and curiosity, true religion and sound theology.

This, then, is the last stronghold of corporate unity. We return to our conviction that such unity is a myth. Here and everywhere the State is no ultimate or genuine unit and has no ultimate or absolute value. While there may be a noble loyalty and an intelligent patriotism, these do not require State domination, or the subservience of human to national ends.

THE BASIS OF STATE UNITY

It has been argued in earlier chapters (*a*) that the function of the State is to provide a number of external aids and conditions for the good life; (*b*) that, owing to its size, the State cannot achieve so easily as smaller associations and groups a spirit of unity and co-operation. On the other hand, it has been admitted (*a*) that States have commanded devoted and single-minded service from some of their best citizens; (*b*) that to many—perhaps to most—of its citizens the idea called by the name of their State —France, Britain, Russia—has been something more positive and more spiritual than the limited and external functions we have attributed to the State would suggest. In fact we have to explain the existence of 'loyalty' and its concentration on an object which would seem to lack the qualities most likely to inspire it.

There is, however, no special puzzle about the devotion and service of public-spirited citizens. Any organisation or institution —a school, a hospital—can command such devotion. It is true, however, that some of these devoted servants of the State do not seem to have thought of it as an instrument for the achievement of security or health or any other of those limited and external ends for which government is necessary. Mazzini, Masaryk, Lenin, Sun Yat-sen—all led their States to goals other than—and many would say higher than—these. But they are only extreme examples of our second problem. How is it that a State can appear in this lofty guise to its citizens?

One answer to this is that the State achieves this appearance by masquerading in borrowed plumage. The Spanish monarch (like others) held the title of His Most Catholic Majesty: Similarly, at least in its early days, the Soviet State was the instrument of a religion, the new religion of communism; it claimed loyalty as having achieved an order based on social justice and destined to be the model and the precursor of world revolution. So in these cases the State could claim the devotion appropriate to the purposes (religious or social) which it claimed to promote.

Identification of the State with religion or economic dogma is uncommon today. Their place has been taken by the 'Nation'. I shall use the word 'nation' in its continental sense, namely to describe the Poles, the Czechs, the Germans as being a group regardless of whether the whole group is included ·in a single State. Thus the Czechs were a nation before they were a State, and some of the German nation were citizens of Rumania and Argentina. This usage is very unnatural to English ears. To us 'nationality' usually means citizenship; nationalism means insistence on the greatness and expansion of one's own State. But, as I wish to use the term, a man might be a German by nationality but a Hungarian citizen. Nationalism will be the theory which bases State unity and State frontiers on national unity and national boundaries, which puts loyalty to the nation above loyalty to the State if the two conflict, and which demands political rights for groups on a national basis. (There are some examples of this usage in English, 'Welsh nationalism' is one.) It is unfortunate to have to attack English usage in this way. But no other word is suitable. 'People' is as misleading. No one would take 'the German people' to include Germans in the Argentine. 'The German Folk' (a translation of *Volk*, which gives the right sense in German) is too consciously archiac. So there is nothing else for it.

Accepting this usage, we can now also use two phrases which in the ordinary usage are unmeaning. To an Englishman Nation and State are two names for the same thing. 'National State' is therefore a vain repetition. But this is a useful phrase for a State based on the common nationality of its citizens, as the successor States of the Habsburg Empire (Czechoslovakia, Yugoslavia, etc.) were and as the Empire was not. Similarly, 'national minority'—meaningless in ordinary usage—is an indispensable term in modern politics to describe citizens of a national State who do not belong to the nationality dominant in that State.

Why have we no word for the German *Volk*? First because we have on the whole escaped the problems of nationality, of which I shall say more below; but also, I think, because we doubt the existence of the unit called the *Volk*. We do not feel inclined to admit that German-speaking people everywhere actually constitute a unit which demands service from its members and instant recognition by the political theorist.

There is also the problem of a criterion. Language is rejected by many nationalists. The Irish were a nation even when almost all of them knew not a word of Erse. The fact that Germany's Jews spoke German did not save them from Hitler and establish them as a part of the German Nation. The use of 'race' as a criterion is wildly unscientific. Indeed, one seems driven back on the view that any group of people who feel they are a nation are a nation. Yet if nothing but a belief unifies the group the belief must be an illusion. Illusions and myths are certainly powerful forces, and believers in them will behave quite differently from non-believers.[1]

But in spite of our general lack of sympathy with this notion of nationhood our own literature illustrates its power of attaching to the machinery of politics an aura of emotion. To illustrate this emotional attachment, I quoted in an earlier chapter[2] Baldwin and Gallacher and an anonymous third person. But it may even then have struck a critical reader that the units to which these three devotees expressed their devotion were none of them States. They were England, Scotland and Ireland (which was still then a part of the United Kingdom). I have not been able to find any similar devotional moods directed on our State—Great Britain and Northern Ireland.

The first result of the creed of national unity is the demand for national independence, i.e. for basing territorial divisions between States on national differences. Mazzini and Masaryk were leaders of their nations before these nations became States; and it was just because they were nations, highly self-conscious and proud, that they insisted on becoming States. The liberation of Italy and Poland and the collapse of the Ottoman and Habsburg Empires culminated in the peace treaties of 1919, in which nationalism dominated the decisions. It took the hard experience of twenty years to raise doubts as to whether this triumph of the national principle was a triumph of progress. It became doubtful whether the Nation-State was an ideal unit to achieve even those

1. For further analysis of the criteria of nationhood, see *Nationalism; a Group Study* (The Royal Institute of International Affairs, 1939).
2. Cf. p. 51.

minimum functions which a State must achieve. Many good Europeans came to regret the disappearance of the Habsburg Empire and to claim that it needed internal reform rather than dissolution. Many others pleaded for confederations or federations in Eastern Europe to undo some of the harm which that dissolution achieved; and practical beginnings had been made in this direction when the Soviet veto descended on them. The argument was that Nation-States—at least in this area (and it is here that nationalism is most rampant)—were unable to provide either security or economic welfare for their citizens and that only larger units could make such provision.

The other corollaries of the identification of nation and State are corollaries of a type shared by those other identifications of the State, with religion or with economic dogma, noted above.

The identification of the State with any non-political purpose or ideal inevitably meets with two difficulties. There will be people outside the State's boundaries who are nevertheless unified through this other bond with the citizens of the State; and there will be people within the State's boundaries who are not unified by this other bond with their fellow-citizens.

Thus if a State is the instrument and expression of the unity of a nation it will tend to claim loyalty from and authority over those of this nation beyond its frontiers. Hitler's claim that German-speaking citizens of Czechoslovakia or Hungary owed a loyalty to him and to Germany overriding their loyalty to the State in which they lived is only a blatant and violent expression of a tendency which is logical and inevitable. The 'three Principles of Sun Yat-sen' were the basic principles of post-war China. The first of these was 'the racial solidarity of the Chinese people'. Students of the Far East had to enquire whether this was a political doctrine. Did it imply control of Tibet and Indo-China? Did it foreshadow Chinese Government action on behalf of the large and influential Chinese population in Malaya? Similarly, so long as the purity of the Lenin-Marxist doctrine was maintained in the USSR, the promotion of world revolution was a primary aim of the Soviet Government, and the Comintern was its natural instrument. It is again a question-mark about the Russia of the future whether the dissolution of the Comintern really closes that era, or whether we must still expect communists in the West to feel their primary loyalty to the Soviet Union, and to draw not only their inspiration but also their orders and their funds from Russia. During the round-up of Soviet spies in Canada, the Russian agent, Igor Gouzenko, stated to the Canadian police: 'It is clear that the Communist Party in democratic countries has changed long ago from a political party into an agency net of the Soviet Government, into a fifth column in these countries to meet a war, into an instrument in the hands of the Soviet Government for creating unrest, provocation, etc.' No evidence comparable to the Canadian Royal Commission Report has been made public in other countries; but that Report contained overwhelming evidence of the complete accuracy of Gouzenko's statement at least so far as the Canadian Communist Party (the 'Labour-Progressive Party') was concerned.

Similarly, in the field of religion, His Most Catholic Majesty felt an obligation to go crusading to protect Christian rights abroad or to interfere on behalf of Roman Catholic minorities in Protestant States—that is, to use the weapons, the resources and the methods of political action for the achievement of the triumph beyond his own frontiers of the religion with which his own power was identified.

All this means is that it is difficult for any one State to heighten the unity within its own borders by harnessing nationality or religion or economic dogma to its chariot without involving itself in an attack on the unity of its neighbour States, amounting at the least to interference with their internal affairs, and tending to the promotion of civil war within them or even to their disruption or absorption into another State.

There is a further stage in this international menace. It is difficult to unify a people on behalf of a nationality, a religion, or an economic creed, without claiming intrinsic superiority for your nation or religion or creed. Again, Hitler was only a good specimen of an ever-present danger. The belief that Germans everywhere owed their main loyalty to the German State led beyond control over German minorities in other States. It led to the *Herrenvolk* or 'Master-Race' doctrine. Then the very existence of Poles or Czechs became not merely a menace to the German minorities in Poland or Czechoslovakia; it became an insult to the German people. Annihilation, assimilation, or subjection was to be the fate of these 'sub-men' who stood across the path of the advancing Aryan race. So also His Most Catholic Majesty was offended if Roman Catholics anywhere were oppressed or their holy places desecrated. But the Roman Catholic religion was even more openly flouted by the existence of solidly Protestant countries with no Roman Catholic minorities at all. Was there

not here a call to an even greater Crusade, requiring the elimina-
tion or conversion or subjugation of such stiff-necked heresy?
Or again, while a good Soviet communist might have a duty to
foment revolution in a country where communism was a living
force, had he not an even greater duty to undermine those solidly
bourgeois countries where communism, except for his support,
would be wholly negligible? Were not such countries a greater
affront to his faith than those others where communism was
well-rooted and required only judicious watering and a place in
the sun?

Nor can we in this country claim to have been wholly free from
these tendencies. In the great days of the Defender of the Faith
we surely felt for united Catholic States such as Spain a greater
hostility just because of their unity than we felt for such divided
States as France. Or, more recently, in our attitude to our
Empire did not our divine right to 'dominion over palm and pine'
carry with it something of the *Herrenvolk* superiority to 'lesser
breeds without the Law'?

The second result of the identification of the State with some
other ideal is internal. Whatever the other ideal may be—A
religion, a nationality, a culture, a language, an economic dogma
—there is likely to be a minority within the State which does not
pursue this ideal and may even pursue a rival. They are likely to
suffer for this. Again the striking example is racial Germany's
treatment of the Jewish race. But again this is only an extreme case
of a common type. Roman Catholic disabilities in Britain, Italy's
treatment of the Germans of the South Tyrol, Poland's persecution of the Ukrainians in Galicia, the purges of the *kulaks* in the
USSR, these were all examples of the same intolerance, inevitable
when the State becomes the instrument of some non-political
purpose. The discrimination may range from murder and torture
down to exclusion from public offices, from professions, or from
positions of trust. It may aim at extermination of the minority
by death or expulsion, at its disappearance by forcible conversion
or the seduction of its children from their parental faith or tongue,
or at its segregation in a position of second-class citizenship. The
essential point is that such intolerance to minorities is a mere
mirror reflection of the State monopoly of some non-political
aim. The evil thing about it is that it is always an attack on inno-
cent people, who happen (normally through no fault of their own)
to have darker skins or longer noses, to speak a different language,
or to practise a different religion from the majority.

No doubt leaders of States often cultivate such monopolies with their eyes open to the consequences. No doubt, also, the immediate instruments of such a policy are often mere brutal sadists. But still the fact remains that the citizens of a State are not generally addicted to cruelty and injustice, except when under the influence of a positive creed which appears to require them.

These, then, are the penalties of attempts to endow the State with 'spiritual' qualities and to make it a suitable object for positive or even mystic devotion.

There is, of course, one other unifier of States—one other god who can shed on government some of his divinity—Mars, the god of war. In war, whether aggressive or defensive, the State inevitably assumes the guise of an idol for which no sacrifice is too great, a power to which no limits can be set. Thus, at the end of a war, there is always a great lamentation about the suddenness with which the spirit of national unity disappears. So also, in the international field, allies fall apart and set to quarrelling. There is nothing surprising or even necessarily regrettable about this. Under the menace of death, national unity and inter-allied unity can reach great heights, because there is a single supreme purpose —victory. If, after peace, inter-allied relations seemed to pursue the same even tenor there would be good grounds for doubt and misgiving. For such unity would almost probably be artificial or superficial, concealing underground tensions and likely to result in a final explosion. It is healthier that the divergences should come out at once and be recognised. Similarly, within the State, it would be a sign of degeneracy if people continued to submit to the dominance of the State in peace as in war. Individual liberties, corporate rights, healthy discord and open opposition, these must all be ruthlessly sacrificed in war. But it was just one of the signs of Germany's pre-1939 degradation that the power and unity of the State were already 'on a war footing' before war came.

Nor does the renunciation of special stimulants to State unity mean that State unity is unattainable. Switzerland and Great Britain (since the departure of Eire) are both examples to show that a high standard of public life and civic loyalty is possible without such aids. Canada is another such example. There is no tendency in Britain to treat the Scots or the Welsh as second-rate citizens or 'sub-men'; nor do similar discriminations of action or attitude assail Italian-speaking Swiss or French Canadians. Peaceful

living together under common laws and under governments
which are not hag-ridden by race, religion, or economic dogma
can produce a unity and a pride of citizenship requiring no artificial stimulants. But this pride and loyalty will not normally be
conspicuous, nor will they normally dominate all other loyalties
in the conscious lives of the citizens. A State of which its ordinary
citizens need not feel ashamed will have its Brights, its Haldanes,
its Mazzinis. (Nazi Germany does not seem to have been able to
retain or to command the loyal service of any honest German of
the first rank in any field of human achievement.) A State which
can call on the services of such men will show two signs of health.
You will not find all its best citizens in State service. The disinterested pursuit of knowledge or beauty will have its servants;
and free associations will have their servants too. It is certainly
unhealthy when (as in the Third Republic in France) politics
comes to be thought of as a dirty trade and despised by men of
honour and independent mind. It is equally unhealthy when all
the best men place government service or politics above all other
avocations. Secondly, State service will be thought of not only
as an honourable profession, but as a special kind of work to
be pursued without ideology and mysticism, without flummery
and cant. And the State itself will appear both to its citizens and
to its officials not as an end but as a means, to be judged always
by its success or failure in achieving those ends which have intrinsic value and own no frontiers or political labels.

We in Britain are sometimes told by our critics that we lack a
dynamic political creed to set against Fascism and Communism;
something to whose services all our children can be educated,
all our young people dedicated, something that can fire the imagination and inspire prophets and priests. (Certainly neither Democracy nor Freedom can fill this bill.) It is a sign of our political
maturity that we have no such creed; it is a pathological symptom
when such a creed sweeps a State; this is monomania, and a
monomaniac may appear a very dynamic person. But real values
have their own dynamism; we have not lacked dynamic minds.
We have had doctors, scientists, artists, lawyers, religious leaders
—and, at need, soldiers, and statesmen—second to none in dynamic drive. But it will be an evil day for us when all these dynam-
isms are directed down a single channel. For this attempt must
fail; the best men would be purged and most of the others terrorised. Only a few would remain who could so adjust their enthusiasm as to serve a new and single master or whom that master

could make his tools. So it is the highest compliment to us that we have no political religion capable, like fascism and communism, of unifying all the lives of all the citizens and of crushing out every activity and every enthusiasm not subservient to its aims.

Appendix

POLITICAL PHILOSOPHY AND THE
SOCIAL SCIENCES

Philosophy was once a name for all human knowledge. This usage has left traces in the titles of professorships (Natural Philosophy, Experimental Philosophy). There is a shop in Edinburgh which sells 'philosophical instruments'; and in a magazine for 1814 there is an account of 'a more philosophical method of making coffee'.

With the growth of specialisation and the perfection of scientific methods, various branches of knowledge developed their own technique and, one after the other, split off from philosophy. Mathematics went first, followed in the seventeenth century by the physical sciences. A hundred years ago economics began its separate development, and within living memory psychology has followed suit. Many political theorists and some philosophers would maintain that political science (or a group of political sciences) is now master of its own field, and that there is no place left in philosophy for the study of the State.

It is to be noted, however, that the separation of philosophy from other sciences was never absolute and that in some cases a reverse tendency has been visible. Russell has brought philosophy and mathematics together again. Whitehead and Eddington have linked physics with philosophy. Philosophers have continued to study problems (e.g. the nature of perception) which fall also in the field of psychology.

How, then, do matters stand with regard to political theory? Firstly, political theory is only a part of social theory, since the State is only one form of association among others. Secondly, there is in social theory a wide field for empirical enquiry by scientific methods. Group psychology—the study of behaviour of men in relation to groups of their fellows—is a part of psychology. Anthropology—the study of social organisation and institutions—is a well-established science. Political Institutions and Economic Organisation have their place as fields of empirical enquiry. Jurisprudence—the examination of the principles common to all legal systems or to the several particular legal systems—has a place of its own. Thus the problem now is not whether there are or should be political or social sciences independent of political philosophy, but whether there is any place left for political philosophy when these sciences have occupied their own fields.

To this question the preceding chapters of this book indicate an answer. The claim made by these chapters is that (whatever the merits of the arguments advanced in them) these arguments are no part of social psychology, anthropology, jurisprudence, or any other empirical science. On the other hand, the fact that these sciences are now well-established is the reason why many topics discussed in previous books on political philosophy find no place here. The most striking omissions are probably discussions of communism and of democracy. To explain this point further I propose to close this Appendix with some observations on theories which might be supposed to involve political philosophy and to indicate why this is not the case. This may also help to remove some confusions in the terms themselves. For example, some men hold that Nazism and Communism are opposed political systems; others hold that there is little to choose between them.

Nazi Germany and the USSR are both examples of totalitarian States, of régimes in which all spheres of life are under government control. Totalitarianism is a political philosophy and, as such, is fully discussed above. Secondly, there are marked resemblances (not surprising, since Hitler borrowed much from Communist methods) between the political institutions of Nazi Germany and of the USSR—the power of the Party and the leader, the political or secret police, the problem of the relation of the Party to the Army, the use of cells and Party observers inside local and functional units. All this constitutes a rich field for the student of comparative political institutions.

The essential difference between Nazism and Communism is not one of political philosophy or of political institutions. It does not lie in the range of political authority or in the way in which it is exercised, but in the purposes for which political power and political machinery are used. Nazism was the application of a totalitarian, single-party, police-State machine to the service of a racial *Herrenvolk* doctrine and an unlimited campaign of territorial aggression ready and willing to use war as an instrument of these aims. The only ideological element in it—the racial theory—is the concern not of philosophers but of ethnologists. In the USSR a very similar machine was applied for the institution and maintenance of new economic arrangements for ownership and control of factories and land, in the interests of the workers. The ideological element here concerns the economist, not the philosopher. The questions whether the arrangements are efficient, whether they really result in maximum benefits to the workers, what amount of control the individual worker in fact exercises—these are empirical questions in the field of economics or political organisation. Thus I hold that the political philosopher, as such, is no more required to hold a view either on the ideology of communism or on its practical application than he is required, *as a philosopher*, to hold a particular view on Free Trade or the merits of Co-operatives. Communism, like capitalism, is not a political philosophy.

It is a further question, both in Nazism and in Communism, whether the totalitarian philosophy is a necessary consequence of the ideology in question. In Nazism there were good grounds for seeing such a connection. The lunacy of the racial doctrine would seem to require lively propaganda for its dupes and rigorous persecution of dissenters; and a programme of territorial aggrandisement, welcoming war as a policy, naturally presupposes a quasi-military organisation to carry it into effect. It is no accident that democracies are peace-loving.

Official Communist doctrine, however, holds that the period of persecution and totalitarian control (the 'dictatorship of the proletariat') is to be transitional only, and is to be replaced by a system of voluntary co-operation between groups of producers, while the State is to 'wither away'.[1] The Soviet Commissar for Education felt it necessary to explain why the Russian State shows no sign of withering away and is in fact more powerful than ever, and in relation to its own subjects more powerful than any. other State now existing. His explanation was that the USSR is ringed round by enemies, and the continued power of the State was necessary to preserve in a hostile world this unique island of economic justice. But there may be other reasons. It is doubtful whether Communism can be maintained without a 'planned economy' and such an economy requires vigorous State control, even if there were no threat or imagined threat from without. It is also doubtful whether the forces against Communism within any State—those elements of individualism which make for private property, family interests, free choice of trade or profession, parental control of children, free criticism and spontaneous association—can be eliminated or sufficiently held in check by education, propaganda and public opinion without continuing governmental control and the ultimate sanction of force. Thus even those who maintain that the triumph of Communism is still the main objective of the USSR and that it has no imperialist or expansionist policy, may still have reason to doubt the official Marxist analysis and to believe that Russia will not be able soon or easily to dispense with the political controls and the political machinery which have established Communism there and have so far maintained it. But once again all this is subject matter for empirical enquiry by the students of Russian history, economic organisation and political institutions.

There are two further terms which require a word of elucidation: dictatorship and fascism. Dictatorship may mean either totalitarianism or one-man rule. There is no doubt that Nazi Germany was a

1. Cf. pp. 104–5.

dictatorship in the first sense; and a main line of defence in the Nuremberg trials has been that it was a dictatorship in the second sense also. The defendants urged that all the main directives of German policy were the direct expression of Hitler's will. They could not oppose him and they bore no responsibility. The possibility, under modern conditions, of one-man government and the methods by which it is carried out concern the student of political institutions.

Fascism is sometimes used simply as a name for Mussolini's régime, sometimes as a term of abuse directed against any government, party, or individual who does not fall in with Soviet wishes. So far as it denotes a distinctive political system it should presumably denote the 'corporative State'. In such a State there is a functional organisation according to trades and professions; but the 'corporations' are, unlike trade unions, dependent on the government and represent all elements in each industry, not the workers only. They are part of the working machinery of the State and in Italy they were firmly controlled by the Fascist Party, which supplied their key officials. Such a system is no more than a complex machinery for totalitarian control; and in fact the Italian corporations never acquired any real vitality or political significance.

Such a system of functional or occupational representation might be added to or substituted for a system of local representation. Divorced from the totalitarianism of a one-party State, the system might then claim to be a new form of democracy. Here we have the theory of the Guild Socialists and the French Syndicalists, a theory upheld in various forms by the Webbs, Professor Laski and Professor Cole. The discussion of these schemes and their possible working is, however, a part of political science.

Democracy is now generally recognised to be the most elusive and ambiguous of all political terms. In its original sense of 'government by the people' it has long been recognised to be an impossible ideal. In one sense it has come to mean a form of government in which the people (or rather the electorate) have the last word because of their ability to confirm their rulers in office or to throw them out. But elections do not make a democracy. Hitler and Kemal held elections and received overwhelming majorities. Yet, by following up this line of thought, we can trace a real difference between forms of government. If the essential attribute of a democracy is its power to accept or reject a government, there must be a genuine possibility of an alternative government. When a dictator holds an election (or when there is a single list of officially sponsored candidates and no other parties may stand) the people who dislike the dictator or the single-list men have either to spoil their ballot-papers or to vote 'No'. But in the unlikely event of a majority of spoilt papers or 'No' votes, the election would be ineffective unless it were followed by a revolution. Moreover, under a totalitarian government (whether dictatorship or single-list) all possible leadership for a revolution is eliminated. Thus it is inevitable that the only organised and public opposition which can claim to succeed a dictator is found in groups of exiles. But that can hardly be called an electoral system or a constitutional machine in which a vote one way requires for its effective implementation a revolution probably engineered from abroad. Thus the elections in totalitarian, one-party (or single-list) States are a farce not because they are conducted under threats and terror (though this is true enough in many cases) but because there is no constitutional alternative to the existing government.

The essential feature of Western democracy and the feature which alone gives any reality to the choice at an election is the existence within the country of an organised opposition recognised as an element in the country's political life, and left so free to develop its programme, its organisation and its resources that it can take over the government at a moment's notice.

There are other features of political life often called 'democratic' which have no direct connection with forms of political organisation.

One is equality—equality of status before the law, or equality of opportunity, or the absence of social or class distinctions especially in relation to privileges, economic or political. In these respects the USSR has a good claim to be more 'democratic' than the Western democracies.

Another feature often held to be democratic is the observation of freedoms or liberties. But the connection of this with democracy as a form of government does not seem to be inevitable. A majority may be tyrannical; and, when it is so, its tyranny is the worst tyranny of all because it is ineluctable. A dictator might be easy-going and allow his subjects a considerable degree of freedom. Thus 'this is a free country' does not necessarily mean 'this is a democratic country' or vice versa. Yet there are some indirect connections between dictatorship and tyranny and also between liberty and democracy. As we have seen, democracy requires the existence of organised opposition, and this in turn requires freedom of association of the press and of public meeting, of discussion and opinion, of conscience and speech.

Some democrats, however, would not rest content with the power to change their government. They demand, as did Rousseau, that the government throughout its tenure of office should be subservient to the people's wishes. They see this is an impossible ideal, but they think any change in that direction is progress. They welcome the referendum and the plebiscite, the detailed publication of party programmes so that the voter should choose between these and not between individuals, the binding of the parliamentary candidate by pledges given at election time that he will support this measure or that, the sensitiveness of the government to public opinion whether expressed in Gallup polls, privately organised 'ballots', demonstrations, press campaigns, hunger marches or squatters' invasions. Whenever any one of these means of pressure succeeds in dictating action by a government, they regard the goal of democracy as brought at least one step nearer. In the strict and original sense of democracy all these tendencies are indubitably democratic. But at this point it becomes doubtful whether all that is democratic is progress, or whether the United Kingdom, for example, is on the road to democracy.

For, ever since Burke's great controversy with his electors at Bristol, it has been an accepted tenet of our constitution that the Member of Parliament is a representative and not a delegate. His duty is to vote according to his conscience in the country's interest as he sees it and not to be tied by instructions or mandates from his constituents. Similarly, our leaders have stood firm against the referendum as liable to destroy all sense of responsibility in the government and to throw power to irresponsible demagogues. We have pitied the Third Republic in France, because the deputies were so tied to their constituencies that effective government was difficult and reasonable taxation impossible. We have criticised the United States constitution because the recurrence at short intervals of presidential or congressional elections tend, as each election looms up, to make popularity, not policy, the touchstone of every political move. Here, then, at all these points, we show doubt as to whether 'democratic' developments are necessarily desirable. But all this makes it doubtful whether 'democracy' can any longer be used with any accuracy or consistency in political theory.

Index